Justin Bieber

Other books in the People in the News series:

Maya Angelou

Glenn Beck

David Beckham

Beyoncé

Sandra Bullock

Fidel Castro

Kelly Clarkson

Hillary Clinton

Stephen Colbert

Suzanne Collins

Miley Cyrus

Ellen Degeneres

Johnny Depp

Zac Efron

Eminem

Roger Federer

50 Cent

Glee Cast and Creators

Jeff Gordon

Al Gore

Tony Hawk

Salma Hayek

Jennifer Hudson

LeBron James

Jay-Z

Derek Jeter

Steve Jobs

Dwayne Johnson

Angelina Jolie

Jonas Brothers

Elena Kagan

Alicia Keys

Kim Jong Il

Coretta Scott King

Ashton Kutcher

Taylor Lautner

Jennifer Lopez

Tobey Maguire

Eli Manning

John McCain

Stephenie Meyer

Barack Obama

Michelle Obama

Apolo Anton Ohno

Danica Patrick

Nancy Pelosi

Katy Perry

Tyler Perry

David Petraeus

Queen Latifah

Daniel Radcliffe

Condoleezza Rice

Rihanna

Alex Rodriguez

Derrick Rose

J.K. Rowling

Shakira

Tupac Shakur

Will Smith

Gwen Stefani

Ben Stiller

Hilary Swank

Taylor Swift

Justin Timberlake

Usher

Serena Williams

Oprah Winfrey

Justin Bieber

By Christine Wilcox

LUCENT BOOKS
A part of Gale, Cengage Learning

GALE
CENGAGE Learning·

Detroit • New York • San Francisco • New Haven, Conn • Waterville, Maine • London

Library of Congress Cataloging-in-Publication Data

Wilcox, Christine.
  Justin Bieber / by Christine Wilcox.
     p. cm. -- (People in the news)
  Includes bibliographical references and index.
  ISBN 978-1-4205-0756-0 (hardcover)
 1. Bieber, Justin, 1994---Juvenile literature. 2. Singers--Canada--Biography--Juvenile
literature. I. Title.
  ML3930.B54W55 2013
    782.42164--dc23
    [B]
                                                                          2012032537

Lucent Books
27500 Drake Rd
Farmington Hills MI 48331

ISBN-13: 978-1-4205-0756-0
ISBN-10: 1-4205-0756-7

Printed in the United States of America
1 2 3 4 5 6 7 16 15 14 13 12

Contents

Foreword   6

Introduction   8
A Teen Idol for the New Millennium

Chapter 1   12
A Rough Start

Chapter 2   24
The Kid Has It All

Chapter 3   36
From YouTube to Superstar

Chapter 4   51
The Image of a Superstar

Chapter 5   64
The Power of the Beliebers

Chapter 6   76
Christian Charity

Notes   84

Important Dates   88

For More Information   90

Index   92

Picture Credits   96

About the Author   96

Fame and celebrity are alluring. People are drawn to those who walk in fame's spotlight, whether they are known for great accomplishments or for notorious deeds. The lives of the famous pique public interest and attract attention, perhaps because their experiences seem in some ways so different from, yet in other ways so similar to, our own.

Newspapers, magazines, and television regularly capitalize on this fascination with celebrity by running profiles of famous people. For example, television programs such as *Entertainment Tonight* devote all their programming to stories about entertainment and entertainers. Magazines such as *People* fill their pages with stories of the private lives of famous people. Even newspapers, newsmagazines, and television news frequently delve into the lives of well-known personalities. Despite the number of articles and programs, few provide more than a superficial glimpse at their subjects.

Lucent's People in the News series offers young readers a deeper look into the lives of today's newsmakers, the influences that have shaped them, and the impact they have had in their fields of endeavor and on other people's lives. The subjects of the series hail from many disciplines and walks of life. They include authors, musicians, athletes, political leaders, entertainers, entrepreneurs, and others who have made a mark on modern life and who, in many cases, will continue to do so for years to come.

These biographies are more than factual chronicles. Each book emphasizes the contributions, accomplishments, or deeds that have brought fame or notoriety to the individual and shows how that person has influenced modern life. Authors portray their subjects in a realistic, unsentimental light. For example, Bill Gates—the cofounder and former chief executive officer of the software giant Microsoft—has been instrumental in making personal computers the most vital tool of the modern age. Few dispute his business savvy, his perseverance, or his technical expertise, yet critics say he is ruthless in his dealings with competitors and driven more by his desire to maintain Microsoft's dominance in the computer industry than by an interest in furthering technology.

In these books, young readers will encounter inspiring stories about real people who achieved success despite enormous obstacles. Oprah Winfrey—one of the most powerful, most watched, and wealthiest women in television history—spent the first six years of her life in the care of her grandparents while her unwed mother sought work and a better life elsewhere. Her adolescence was colored by pregnancy at age fourteen, rape, and sexual abuse.

Each author documents and supports his or her work with an array of primary and secondary source quotations taken from diaries, letters, speeches, and interviews. All quotes are footnoted to show readers exactly how and where biographers derive their information and provide guidance for further research. The quotations enliven the text by giving readers eyewitness views of the life and accomplishments of each person covered in the People in the News series.

In addition, each book in the series includes photographs, annotated bibliographies, timelines, and comprehensive indexes. For both the casual reader and the student researcher, the People in the News series offers insight into the lives of today's newsmakers—people who shape the way we live, work, and play in the modern age.

A Teen Idol for the New Millennium

Each generation has its teen idol. From Frank Sinatra to Justin Timberlake, teen idols of every era have won the hearts of their young fans. The latest teen sensation is Canadian singer Justin Bieber, who exploded onto the music scene in 2009 with his platinum-selling album, *My World*. His fans, who call themselves "Beliebers," number in the tens of millions, and "Bieber Fever" is bigger than Beatlemania of the 1960s—the widespread fervor over British rock group the Beatles. Beliebers track Justin Bieber's every move online and flock to his appearances, sometimes turning up in such numbers that they can overwhelm security and put themselves in danger. In 2012, when Justin announced a secret show in Oslo, Norway, tens of thousands of Beliebers flooded the streets, almost shutting down the city. Several were injured in the crowd and had to be hospitalized.

The Perfect Fantasy Boyfriend

What causes Bieber Fever? Justin Bieber is undeniably talented— by the age of twelve, he had taught himself to play four instruments and had performed with a professional jazz band. He sings about idealized, romantic love, a preoccupation of tween and teen girls. He has charisma and star presence but is not so practiced that his "cool" seems fake; even after being in the spotlight for three years, Justin can sound a little awkward in an interview.

Performer Justin Bieber taught himself to play instruments at a young age. His youth, looks, talent, and nice-guy image have made him the perfect fantasy boyfriend for his young fans.

He has an inspiring story: born into poverty to an unwed teen mother, young Justin had no real aspirations to be famous until a promoter stumbled across a video of him singing in a local talent show.

But the most appealing aspect of Justin Bieber—at least according to his fans—is his "cuteness." His features are soft and slightly feminine, making him appear younger than he really is. The iconic hairstyle that he wore until 2011, a forward-swooping bob, is an updated version of the "mop top" worn by the Beatles at the beginning of their career, and it contributed to his youthful appearance. All of this makes him a safe and nonthreatening fantasy boyfriend for an age group that can feel overwhelmed by their burgeoning sexuality. Also, because he was just a normal kid singing in his bedroom until 2008, his fans can identify with him. They believe Justin Bieber is just like them.

Social Networking Superstar

Justin Bieber has been hailed as the first superstar of the digital age. In 2008 Atlanta-based music promoter Scott "Scooter" Braun discovered Justin on the social media site YouTube. Braun was so impressed by the twelve-year-old's voice, appearance, and stage presence that he tracked him to the small town of Stratford, Ontario, and eventually became his manager.

At the time the music industry did not sign unknown teen singers. Stars like Miley Cyrus and Justin Timberlake began their careers as television actors, or they were hand-selected for industry-created musical groups, like Timberlake's band, 'N Sync. On the other hand, Justin had nothing but a few dozen homemade videos that he posted on YouTube. But by the time he approached the music industry, those videos had been viewed millions of times, and his fan base was growing exponentially. With the help of Braun and R&B star Usher Raymond, Justin convinced a recording label that his Internet fan base could launch him to superstardom.

The "Beliebers"

Justin Bieber's fans are a cultural phenomenon in their own right. Millions strong, they organize on social networking sites to wield unprecedented power over the star's career. They have bought out his singles and albums en masse on the day of release to launch them to the top of the *Billboard* charts. They have organized campaigns to push him to top of Twitter (as of September 2012, Justin was second only to Lady Gaga, who had more than 29 million Twitter followers to his 28 million). They have even gone so far as to send death threats (via Twitter or e-mail) to anyone who interferes with his career.

Fan clubs are nothing new, but Justin's fans grew up in the age of social media, and they are the first mega-fan club to be able to communicate with each other at all times of the day, from all places on the planet. Their loyalty to Justin comes from a sense of ownership—many claim they have supported him since he first began posting videos in 2008. Justin reciprocates their loyalty by tweeting to his fans several times a day, thanking them for their support and sharing the details of his life. He hugs them in crowds, gives them free tickets, pays them surprise visits, and, during each show, serenades one lucky girl onstage.

A Role Model for His Generation

Justin Bieber is determined to be a role model for his fans. His mother, Pattie Mallette, is a born-again Christian, and she believes that God gave her son this opportunity so that he could morally influence and inspire his generation. Justin shares her religious beliefs, though he rarely discusses them. Instead, he chooses to lead by example. He does not smoke or do drugs. He participated in a campaign to stop teens from texting while driving, and he came out against bullying as part of the It Gets Better project, in which celebrities (and regular people) share personal stories of bullying to help kids realize that one day they will move past that hurt. He has also built a charity component into every business deal he has ever made.

Part of Justin's success is due to his determination to always improve himself. "There's no point in doing this if I'm not going to be the best," he told *Complex* magazine. "I give up a personal life. I give up my friends and family to pursue what I love and to make my fans happy. Why would I give up so much to be just another singer?"[1] His fans find his hard work inspiring, and they see Justin as an example of what can happen when you are determined to make your dreams come true.

Chapter 1

A Rough Start

Justin Bieber's childhood was typical in many respects—he loved sports, often played the class clown, and generally stayed out of trouble. Even now, as one of the biggest stars of the twenty-first century, he is a down-to-earth teenager with a healthy mix of confidence and humility. But Justin had a difficult start in life. His mother, Pattie Mallette, gave birth to him when she was just a teenager. As a single mother, she barely had enough money to take care of her son. But with great determination and the help of her family and her church, she made sure that Justin had what he needed and was surrounded by people who loved him.

Mallette's own story is remarkable. Understanding how she went from being a wild teenager to a resourceful young mother helps explain how Justin was able to avoid repeating his mother's mistakes and grow up to be a remarkably grounded young man.

"You Just Sort of Take It and Hide"

Patricia Mallette grew up in the Canadian province of Ontario, which sits above the Great Lakes on the U.S.-Canada border. Mallette had a difficult childhood. She describes her home as broken, filled with tension and pain. Her biological father abused her mother, and he died when Mallette was three years old. (Her mother later married Bruce Dale, who became Mallette's stepfather.) Her five-year-old sister was hit by a car and died, a tragedy that haunted the family. These hardships would have been difficult for anyone to deal with, but Mallette herself also

Justin Bieber's mother, Pattie Mallette, raised her son as a single mom, working hard to give Justin a good and loving upbringing.

went through a horrible ordeal as a child. Between the ages of five and ten, she was sexually abused.

Like many abused children, she never reached out for help or told anyone. "It was just sort of known that you don't say anything," she explained. "I didn't want to ruffle the feathers and cause trouble and hurt people, so, you just sort of take it and hide."[2] Keeping such a terrible secret took its toll. Her childhood years were filled with pain and anger, and she had no one to help her overcome it. Mallette has yet to publicly reveal the identity of her abuser, preferring to keep those details private.

When Mallette became a teenager, she began to act out the pain she held inside of her. She was deeply unhappy at home and did not get along with her mother or stepfather. At fourteen she began experimenting with drugs and alcohol, and she admits that she was often high or drunk at school. She began to associate with a wild crowd—older teenagers who liked to party. At fifteen she left home and moved in with four male friends who shared a house. While there Mallette abused alcohol and drugs, experimented with sex, and even committed crimes. She was trying to experience some sort of wild pleasure to cover up the pain of her past abuse. But her life was spinning out of control, and she had no idea how to get help.

At seventeen Mallette hit bottom. She felt so hopeless that it seemed to her that the only way to escape her pain was to commit suicide. She decided she would let herself be hit by a car—the same way her sister had died. On the day she tried to kill herself, Mallette stood on the curb of a busy street, spotted a truck speeding toward her, and stepped in front of it, timing her actions so she would be killed instantly. Luckily, the vehicle swerved down a side street, and Mallette was not hit. Instead, she was taken to the mental health ward of the local hospital and placed on suicide watch.

Becoming a Single Mom

While in the hospital Mallette was visited by only one friend— the director of a local youth center. The man, whose name was John, brought her outside food and talked with her, trying to give her some comfort. John was a Christian, and he told her about Christianity while she ate. Mallette did not believe God existed, but she listened anyway, happy for the company.

During one of their talks, John suggested that, since Mallette had tried to commit suicide and did not seem to want her own life, maybe she should give her life over to God. This statement made an impression. After John left that day, she decided to pray, asking God to forgive her for her sinful actions and tell her what to do with her life. And because she still was not sure that God existed, she asked God to give her a sign that he was real.

It was then that Mallette had what she describes as a direct encounter with God. She closed her eyes and had a vision of her heart opening and being filled with bright, sparkling dust, which she believed was God's presence or love. Once her heart was completely filled up, it turned a pure, brilliant white, which meant to her that her sins were forgiven and her heart was made new. "I could feel something wash over me and I just started weeping," she remembers. "He had forgiven me, and I was clean, and he was real!"[3] Mallette was ecstatic. She immediately called John and told him what had happened. He rushed back to the hospital with a Bible and explained that, according to Christianity, she had been saved.

With her newfound faith, Mallette made several positive changes in her life. She stayed away from her former friends and their partying lifestyle for a while. She joined a nondenominational evangelical church that had an emphasis on music, and she learned how to design websites so she could get a good job. But about six months later, Mallette drifted back into her old habits. She began to go to parties again and started dating Jeremy Bieber, a local boxer and construction worker who had a police record for assault. Bieber was also in his late teens and was not ready to settle down. Soon after starting a relationship with Bieber, Mallette became pregnant.

It was then, with baby Justin on the way, that Mallette renewed her commitment to her faith and turned her life around for good. She was embarrassed to return to her church as a pregnant teen, but she mustered up her courage and went back—and was pleased to find that the church members welcomed her return. She and Bieber moved in together and made plans to get married. "I wanted to make sure I gave him everything, that I would be the best that I could be for him," she said of her unborn baby. "I knew he needed stability in his life, and God really gave me a lot of strength."[4] Mallette was determined that Justin would be brought up in a happy home and not repeat the mistakes she made as a teenager.

"We Were Definitely Less Privileged"

Justin Drew Bieber was born on March 1, 1994, at St. Joseph's Hospital in London, Ontario, about 40 miles (64km) from his mother's hometown of Stratford. As they had planned, Mallette

After his birth in nearby London, Ontario, Justin Bieber was raised in his mother's hometown of Stratford.

and Bieber tried to raise their son together, but it soon became clear that Bieber was not ready for the responsibility of being a full-time father. Ten months after Justin was born, the two teenagers decided it was not working out and broke off their engagement. Bieber began to work out of town on construction jobs, and Mallette found herself an unemployed, unwed teen mother.

Mallette began receiving public assistance from the Canadian government. She and baby Justin moved into subsidized housing—that is, housing that is less expensive because it is partially paid for by the government. The basement apartment they rented was infested with rodents. "That place was really dirty," Justin remembers. "We had mousetraps everywhere because there were mouses—uh, mice—in the house. I didn't have a real bed.

Stratford, Ontario

Stratford is a small city in southwestern Ontario, Canada, with a population of about thirty thousand. It was named after Stratford-upon-Avon in the United Kingdom, the birthplace of William Shakespeare.

Apart from being the hometown of Justin Bieber, Stratford is most well known for its annual Shakespeare Festival and lively arts scene. The Stratford

Actors perform a scene from one of William Shakespeare's plays during the Shakespeare Festival. Stratford, Ontario is most well-known for this annual festival, which draws theater-goers from far and wide.

Summer Music Festival features indoor and outdoor performances by Canadian performers and international artists, many of whom perform outdoors in downtown Stratford. In addition, Nathan McKay, one of Justin's early musical mentors, organizes the annual Stratford Kinsman Blues & Rib Festival held each June.

Notable past and present residents include Thomas Edison, who worked as a telegraph operator at Stratford's railway station; world music artist Loreena McKennitt; composer and musician Richard Manuel of The Band; and international operatic singers James Westman and Roger Honeywell.

To accommodate the influx of Justin Bieber fans, the Stratford Tourism Alliance created a walking tour of Bieber's popular childhood haunts. A map can be downloaded at www.visitstratford.ca/justin.

I slept on a blue pull-out couch in my room."[5] Mallette worked a series of low-paying jobs to supplement the government assistance she was receiving: She designed websites, taught computer classes, and worked as a receptionist. Still, feeding herself and her son was sometimes a problem. "We didn't have anything in the fridge, except maybe luncheon meat for school and macaroni and cheese,"[6] Justin remembers. When money was particularly tight, the family had to visit the local food pantry, where they received food donations for free. Mallette's church was also supportive. Church members brought groceries without being asked, and one church member even gave them a car.

By working hard and asking for help, Mallette made sure Justin did not suffer the stresses and disruptions that often come along with living near the poverty line. Her hard work paid off. "I grew up—I wouldn't say poor but we were definitely less privileged," Justin remembers. "Sometimes I would go over to my friend's house and they had more, like, toys and stuff. But I had a roof over my head."[7] Though it was not easy for Justin to grow up without much money, his mother made sure he always had everything he needed.

It Takes a Village

People sometimes say it takes a village to raise a child, and this was indeed true of Justin's upbringing—family and friends came together to help Mallette raise her son. Justin was a very active child, and his mom needed all the help she could get. "When he was a baby he didn't stop, ever," she remembers. "Always been hyper, still hyper. He was a lot of work."[8] Her mother and stepfather, Diane and Bruce Dale, lived nearby, and they were thrilled to have a grandchild. When he was not in preschool, Justin stayed with his grandparents while his mom was at work. Bruce and Diane even fixed up a room in their home for Justin, decorating the walls with motifs of his beloved hockey team, the Toronto Maple Leafs.

Justin and his grandfather bonded right away and became very close. "He was always with Justin, every day," remembers Diane. "If he wasn't with him he'd be talking to him."[9] In fact, Bruce treated Justin like he was one of his own children. "I tried to see

Growing up, Justin admired artists such as Michael Jackson, one of the artists his mother often listened to on the radio.

that he never went without," he remembers. "If he needed some money he got it. Just generally, if they were going somewhere he knew that I would be there with him."[10] Bruce acted as a second father to his grandson, supporting him and being a stable male figure in his life.

Some of Justin's fondest memories are of spending summers with his grandparents at a fishing and hunting club on Star Lake, one of the many lakes in Ontario. He especially enjoyed fishing early in the morning with his grandfather and great-grandfather and spending the evenings around the campfire. Those summers were special to Justin, and they helped him appreciate the bonds of family.

Early Musical Talent

Justin's mother first noticed he had musical talent when he was two years old, banging on a kitchen chair in time with the music on the radio. His timing and rhythm were remarkable—many adults would be hard-pressed to match it. Mallette was a singer and loved music; she always had the radio on in their apartment, listening to Boyz II Men and Michael Jackson—artists that Justin admires to this day. She had many friends who were musicians, and she often had people over for jam sessions in her living room. She and Justin also attended church band rehearsals, hanging out with the band while they were jamming or rehearsing.

One of the musicians, Nathan McKay, let Justin play with the percussive noisemakers during rehearsals. McKay had gone to school with Mallette and was a longtime family friend. He was stunned at how talented Justin was. McKay said that Justin "would wander up to the stairs right in front of the drum kit and just stare at Dan, the drummer in the band at the time, and he would just be mesmerized, and he would grab a pair of drum-sticks and he'd start hitting the stairs. And everybody noticed that his timing was amazing. Where does this talent come from? Does he play drums? Man, you better get that kid a kit."[11] Mallette took this advice and got Justin a child-sized plastic drum kit, and with the help of her friends, Justin became an accomplished drummer by the time he was five.

The *Djembe*

One present that Justin received during his family's Christmas gift-giving tradition was a *djembe*. A *djembe* is a traditional African drum meant to be played with bare hands instead of drumsticks. Though his family could not afford drum lessons or to upgrade his child-sized drum kit to a professional one, they hoped the *djembe* would allow him to continue to play drums in at least some capacity.

The *djembe* stands about 2 feet (61cm) tall and is designed to be played while sitting. The body of the drum is made of hardwood, and the drumhead is made of rawhide. It is tuned by a series of ropes attached to the drumhead, which can be tightened or loosened to change the

For Christmas one year Justin received a traditional African drum called a djembe, and he taught himself to play.

drum's tone and volume. When tuned for solo performances, its volume can rival a jackhammer.

The *djembe* can produce a variety of sounds. *Djembe* players use different techniques to create three basic sounds: bass, tone, and slap. *Djembefolas* can produce up to twenty-five distinct sounds. Some musicians who have performed with the *djembe* and helped make it popular as a modern instrument are the Beatles, the Grateful Dead, and Paul Simon.

Christmas

Christmas was a big affair in the Dale household. The family looked forward to Diane's delicious turkey dinner, after which they would gather in the living room for a gift exchange. Bruce had children from a previous marriage, so that family joined in the celebration as well. Everyone placed a wrapped gift in a pile and played a game with dice to see who would choose a present first—or "steal" a present from someone else. It was a wonderful tradition for a large, extended family that did not have the resources to buy a present for each person.

Even though Justin sometimes wished for a "perfect" family instead of the blended and extended family he had, he learned a lot about tolerance and acceptance. "In our family, all the kids know they're loved, and, for the most part, everybody's able to just get over themselves and be cool. You just love and accept everybody as they are. You forgive others and hope that others will forgive you."[12] Justin's family taught him to tolerate differences and accept people for who they are—values that fit in with his mom's Christian beliefs.

The Best Father He Could Be

In those early years Justin's father, Jeremy Bieber, was often working out of town and could not spend much time with his son. He did see Justin whenever possible, bringing him along to the gym where he trained as a boxer, and later teaching Justin how to defend himself from bigger kids who might bully him because he was small. Bieber also stayed on friendly terms with Mallette, and she remembers him as a good father. "[Justin's] dad was working in another province some of the time, but when he saw him, it was great. He's a good dad. He'll discipline him when he needs to discipline him and love him when he needs to love him."[13] Though Bieber had to take work where he could find it to support himself and help support Justin, he was committed to spending time with his son whenever he could.

Some reporters have speculated that Bieber's involvement in his son's life came only after Justin achieved fame, but Justin himself discredits this. "My dad was away at work a lot of the time, and, yeah, that sucked for me sometimes," Justin admits. "It sucked for him, too. But in life you realize that the world's not perfect and if it had been up to us, we'd have been together all the time."[14] Bieber was there for Justin when he needed his father, and Mallette made sure that her differences with Bieber did not get in the way of their relationship as father and son.

A Formidable Talent

Although Justin's childhood was far from perfect, it was filled with love and support. Mallette was honest with Justin about her wild youth, wanting him to learn from her mistakes so he would not repeat them when he was a teenager. She also encouraged Justin to explore his interests at his own pace.

From the beginning there was something unusual about Justin. His natural talent for music was formidable. Like many mothers, Mallette thought her son was special, but she assumed his interest in music would turn out to be nothing more than an enjoyable hobby. She never dreamed how far his talent would take him.

Chapter 2

The Kid Has It All

It takes more than talent to become a superstar. Many people have a natural gift for music—learning to play or to sing is easy for them, and they have an intuitive understanding of how music works. But without putting in thousands and thousands of hours of practice, budding musicians will never reach their full potential. For that they need drive and determination, lots of energy, and a healthy interest in competition. To be star performers, however, they need one more thing—stage presence. A star has to love getting up in front of people and must know how to connect with an audience.

During his school years, Justin discovered he had all of these characteristics: talent, drive, a love of competition, and natural stage presence. Still, nobody—including Justin—imagined that a kid from a small town in Canada could become one of the biggest superstars in the world.

"He Wouldn't Pass the Ball"

Justin started first grade at Jeanne Sauvé Catholic School in Stratford, a French immersion public elementary school. He had many friends at Jeanne Sauvé, but he met his best friends when he joined the local ice hockey league. He was small for his age, and he was worried about being labeled a "French geek"[15] by the other boys on the team, who went to an English-speaking public school. But he was fast and had great reflexes, and soon found himself with two new best friends, Ryan Butler and Chaz Somers.

Justin joined an ice hockey league in elementary school. He was a competitive player and enjoyed the sport. He especially enjoyed winning.

Justin excelled at sports, and it was a wonderful outlet for his abundant energy. Sports also helped his grandparents manage their active grandson, who lived part-time at their house. "If he didn't have sports," his grandmother commented, "he would have gotten into trouble, maybe, because he was just so go-go-go-go, all the time."[16] His grandparents supported Justin's interest in sports, which extended to basketball, soccer, and cross-country running, and his room in their home was soon filled with trophies and ribbons. He remembers that there was always a family member in the stands—usually Bruce Dale. Because Justin had this support, he never felt intimidated in front of a crowd. In fact, he found that he liked to show off his talents.

Ryan's father, Martin Butler, was the boys' soccer coach for several years. He soon noticed that Justin had a very strong competitive streak, as well as a bad habit of showing off on the field.

Canada: A Bilingual Country

French immersion is an educational method used in Canada that teaches English-speaking students entirely in French. Justin Bieber received his elementary education at a public French immersion school, where all subjects were taught in French. As a result, he is bilingual. As a child, Justin often translated for his great-grandfather, who was French Canadian and did not speak English.

Both French and English are official languages in Canada. Canada is part of the United Kingdom, but about 30 percent of the population identify themselves as French Canadian, an ethnic group descended from French colonists. They reside primarily in Quebec, where French is the native tongue of 80 percent of the population.

"He would not release the ball," Butler said of Justin. "It's the same with hockey, he wouldn't pass the puck. In soccer he wouldn't pass the ball. When he did, it worked out, it was great. I had to stress to him that making the goal was as important as scoring the goal."[17] Justin was very close with the Butlers, but the lesson Martin Butler tried to teach him—to put the team in front of the individual—did not stick. While Justin did learn to be a good team player, he loved competition and he loved to win. For Justin, being the best at something—whatever it may be—was a primary motivation.

A Self-Taught Musician

Just as Justin's interest in hockey led him to play many other sports, his interest in the drums led him to try other instruments. By the time he started school at Jeanne Sauvé, Justin's musical

Justin's parents encouraged his interest in music. His dad introduced Justin to the music of guitar legend Jimi Hendrix.

interests had expanded to include the piano and the guitar. (Later he taught himself to play the trumpet.) Pattie Mallette still entertained her musical friends in her living room, and occasionally even Justin's father was invited over for an impromptu jam session. Jeremy Bieber taught his son to play classic rock songs like "Smoke on the Water" by Deep Purple. He also introduced him to the music of guitar legends like Jimi Hendrix and Eddie Van Halen.

Family friend Nathan McKay was also one of Justin's early musical mentors. McKay commented that Justin had the "ability to imitate at a very young age. He would see somebody with a talent—it didn't matter if it was sports or music or even just doing tricks—[and] he could adapt really quickly and then excel at it."[18] This talent—to learn by example, rather than from instruction—is crucial for self-taught musicians. It involves watching and listening carefully, both to the person you are trying to imitate and then to yourself. Justin had this ability, and his competitive nature motivated him to persist and become a better and better musician.

Along with a gift for imitation, Justin had an intuitive talent for music. As he experimented with piano and guitar, he instinctively knew when notes harmonized and when they did not—the same way he instinctively knew how to play along with a song on the drums. He says about the piano, "I could feel it when the chords and melody didn't fit together, the same way you can feel it when your shoes are on the wrong feet. I just kept poking and experimenting until the notes fit together the way I wanted them to."[19] Many children become discouraged by the complexity of the piano or the discomfort of pressing down guitar strings with small fingers, and they must be forced to practice. But to Justin, playing music was an enjoyable challenge. Just as he was driven to perfect his skills in sports, he practiced his instruments until he was an accomplished musician. Playing music was just another way for him to have fun.

Busking on the Sidewalk

One night when Justin was about eight years old, McKay came over to babysit while Justin's mother went out for the evening. McKay, who was active in Stratford's music scene, decided to let Justin try his hand at busking. *Busking* is when musicians play for tips in a public place. From April to November, people come from all over the world to attend the Stratford Shakespeare Festival, and local musicians like McKay earn extra money by busking for tourists.

That night McKay brought Justin to a popular busking spot and let him watch the musicians play. Then he set Justin up on a bench with his *djembe*. As Justin played the African drum, people stopped to listen, impressed that a small boy could play so well. Before long, Justin had earned twenty-six dollars—the first time he had made money performing for an audience. He was thrilled. At midnight Mallette called McKay, wondering where her son was so long after his bedtime. She was both surprised and excited to

When he was eight years old, Justin began busking, or
street performing, in front of the Avon Theater in Stratford.
He met other musicians and enjoyed the public attention
that busking brought.

Busking

Busking—the practice of performing in public for tips—has been around for centuries. The word *busk* is derived from the Spanish word *buscar*, which means "to seek." Before recording devices were invented, busking was the most common way for entertainers to earn a

Entertainers who practice busking perform in public for tips. Musicians are among those who engage in busking.

living and "seek" fame. Buskers are also known as street performers, minstrels, or troubadours. Street performance is not limited to music; dancers, puppeteers, magicians, jugglers, and poets all perform for the public in exchange for gratuities.

There are three types of busking. Circle shows are performances with a distinct beginning and end, and they tend to draw a crowd. After the performance, the entertainer will gather donations, often by passing a hat. Circle shows work best for street theater, and walk-by acts are more common with musicians, who provide outdoor ambient music for passersby. Café busking is usually performed indoors. A musician provides musical entertainment for a venue and is paid in tips. Billy Joel is known for spending a stint as a café busker and describing the experience in his song "Piano Man."

learn that Justin had actually made money. Up until that point, Mallette had not considered that her son's interest in music was anything more than a way to have fun.

From that point on, Justin honed both his musical and performance skills by busking on the streets of Stratford. "Between [the ages of] eight and twelve, you know, he really had a lot of time to rehearse, here in the city," McKay explained. "For those people who think Justin is an overnight success, he really paid his dues over those four years. … Schoolgirls often didn't want to go into the theater because they wanted to catch every moment of Justin's performance on the Avon Theater steps. He's definitely had a lot of practice."[20] Busking also put Justin in contact with other musicians. Even though he did not sing in public until he was twelve, a lot of people were already impressed by his musical talent.

The Justin Bieber Benefit Concert

After Justin's success busking, McKay decided it was time that Justin had an adult drum set. He talked with his band, and they decided to organize a benefit concert for Justin, hoping to raise enough money to buy him a Pearl drum kit. They decided to call it the Justin Bieber Benefit Concert and held it at a local bar, charging five dollars per person at the door. Justin played drums at the concert. McKay said, "When we were preparing him for his show, he had to learn four jazz standards. For an eight year old to play jazz was quite difficult, but he was up for it."[21] Justin did well, and the benefit was a huge success. They made enough money to buy Justin the Pearl drum kit he wanted, which he kept at his grandparents' house. "He'd go into the furnace room and bang on those drums like you couldn't believe," Bruce Dale remembers. "And the worst part of it was he was good."[22]

Justin was so good that McKay's band invited him to join them at several more gigs. Justin was small for his age, and it was hard to see him behind the huge drum kit—in fact, it was hard to tell anyone was sitting behind the drum kit at all. When the audience realized that a little kid with his hat on backward was playing drums—and playing well—they were astonished. The novelty of hearing a young boy play with an adult band caused audiences to cheer and applaud. Justin was getting a taste of fame, and he loved it.

Abundant Energy

In the seventh grade Justin began attending Stafford Northwestern Secondary School, an English-speaking middle school. His hockey mates, Ryan Butler and Chaz Somers, also attended the school, and the three friends could now spend more time together. Not many of Justin's peers knew that he was into music, and they saw him as just a regular kid. He kept his musical talents under wraps to avoid being teased. "Volunteering the information that you sometimes stand in front of the bathroom mirror pretending to be Michael Jackson and singing 'Rockin' Robin' into a blow-dryer," said Justin, "that's something you can and probably should keep to yourself."[23] Some of his close friends knew that he played piano and guitar, but they did not know he also liked to sing—and could sing well.

As kids often do—especially the active ones—Justin got into plenty of trouble. His abundant energy was a wonderful asset when it came to practicing sports or music, but it could also land him in trouble at school. "Outside, I'd be showing off on my skateboard, kicking a soccer ball around, or just stirring things up with Chaz and Ryan, and it was hard to turn that off in the building,"[24] Justin remembers. He got into trouble for laughing in class, singing in the library, and dancing in the hallways, and often found himself sent to the principal's office. Once, he got so frustrated that, instead of going to the school office, he walked home to his grandparents' house. That incident got him in trouble twice—first with the principal, whom Justin had to face when his grandfather took him back to school—and then with his mother, who was furious when she learned what Justin had done.

He also got into the occasional schoolyard brawl, but because his father had taught him how to defend himself, he did not have much of a problem from bullies. He also got into his fair share of trouble with Ryan and Chaz. On one occasion he and his friends snuck out at two o'clock in the morning and were picked up by the police. His mother grounded him for several weeks, but she let him keep practicing his instruments. It was important to her that he directed his energy productively. Music was always an activity she encouraged.

Stratford Star

Justin's mother supported his interest in music. But she had no idea he was interested in singing in front of people until he asked her if he could try out for Stratford Star. Stratford Star is a talent competition modeled after the television show *American Idol* and hosted each year by the Stratford Youth Centre. Kids from ages twelve to eighteen audition for the competition, and only the most talented are chosen to compete. Those chosen sing in front of an audience in a series of elimination rounds and are judged by people from the local music scene in Stratford.

In 2007 many people in the United States and Canada were fans of *American Idol*, and Justin was no exception. His friends—the ones who knew he played music—told him that he should be on the show, but he knew he was too young. Singers could not audition for *American Idol* unless they were at least sixteen, and Justin was only twelve. So he did the

The city of Stratford had a local version of the popular U.S. competitive singing show, "American Idol." Called the Stratford Star, young Justin was eager to take part in the competition in 2007.

next best thing—he asked his mother if he could compete in Stratford Star.

Mallette was worried. "I didn't know he actually wanted to sing in front of people until he came to me at twelve and said 'I want to try out for Stratford Idol.' I said, 'There's only ten people going to make it, it's ages twelve to eighteen, you're only twelve, you've never had any singing lessons and you've never sang in front of anybody before.'"[25] She was afraid that if Justin was not chosen to compete, he might become discouraged and give up on music entirely. But Justin was insistent. He was not afraid of performing—he figured it was a lot like playing sports in front of spectators. He just wanted to see what it was like, singing in front of an audience. So Mallette helped him prepare background tracks for his songs and pick out clothes to wear.

As it turned out, Mallette had no reason to worry—Justin was picked as one of the ten finalists. After he got through the first few rounds, he sang "3 AM" by Matchbox 20 and got a good response from the audience. The response got more enthusiastic at his next performance, when he sang "Fallin'" by Alicia Keys. For the final round, he decided to sing "Respect" by Otis Redding, as it was performed by Aretha Franklin. Since his confidence was bolstered after the success of his last two performances, he was eager to get up onstage.

He never expected what happened next. It seemed that word of Justin's talent had spread through Stratford, and many people had come to the performance to hear him sing—including a group of teenage girls. When Justin got up onstage, they began to scream. "I got up and sang my little eighth-grade butt off, thinking it was possibly the greatest moment of my entire life," he remembers. "Those girls in the back were into the number, swaying and clapping. I was feeding off the energy and it felt great."[26] Justin discovered that he thrived on performing and that he could make a connection with the audience. He could even make mistakes—like dropping his microphone—and not lose his confidence. He was a natural performer, and the audience loved him.

Justin did not win the Stratford Star competition; he came in third. The performers who won second and first place were eighteen and had studied voice professionally. Although his grandfather had taught Justin to be a good loser, and he was the first to shake the winner's hand, he was very disappointed. "A little chunk of my heart fell out and rolled under the piano," he remembers. "I wanted to win. I mean, if you don't care about winning the competition, why show up? I know that sounds harsh but I just love competition so much that I'm sometimes very hard on myself."[27] Still, losing the competition did not discourage Justin. He wanted to perform again.

Justin's mother had taken videos of his performance and put them on YouTube. Justin assumed that only his friends and family would see the videos, and that his life would go on as it always had—practicing, playing sports, going to school, hanging out with his friends. Maybe someday, when he was older, he would make a living playing music, but there was plenty of time to think about that later.

Ready for the Big Time

Many famous musicians say that their success is due to being at the right place at the right time. But they also stress that when an artist's lucky break comes, he or she has to be ready. By the time he was twelve, Justin Bieber was ready. His natural talent and competitive streak had driven him to become an accomplished musician. His abundant energy and his love of being in the spotlight made him pursue opportunities like busking and competing in a talent show—opportunities that few children (and adults) are brave enough to attempt. What is even more remarkable is that nobody pushed Justin to practice or perform. Self-taught and driven by a true love of music, he pushed himself.

With practice and hard work, twelve-year-old Justin Bieber had become a skilled and dynamic performer. Now all he needed was a little luck. That luck came knocking a few months later.

Chapter 3

From YouTube to Superstar

Many people believe that after Justin performed in the Stratford Star talent competition, he became an overnight success. In fact, it took nearly two years for Justin to become famous. The story of his rise to fame hinges on his innovative use of new social media and networking sites like YouTube and Twitter. By reaching out directly to kids his own age, Justin soon amassed a loyal fan base millions strong. In the process he forever changed the way the music industry markets its artists.

Singing on the Street

After Justin had a taste of what it was like to sing for an audience, he was hooked. As the tourists poured into Stratford for the annual Shakespeare Festival, he decided to take his guitar to the popular busking spots and try singing. He set up on the steps of the Avon Theater, an area that had great acoustics and a lot of foot traffic. Justin wanted some extra pocket money, and he hoped he would get a good response from the crowd. To his surprise, on his first day he earned over two hundred dollars.

His mother was thrilled. She suggested Justin start a college fund, but Justin had other ideas. He wanted to take his mom to Disney World. Together they decided they would save for both—college and a family trip. Pattie Mallette was nervous about Justin being alone on the sidewalk with so much cash, so she and

Justin's grandfather took turns parking across the street while Justin played.

Justin became a popular addition to the street musicians in Stratford. When he played he always drew a crowd. People in the apartments across the street opened their windows to listen to his music, and nearby businesses liked it when he played because tourists lingered near their stores. Justin knew lots of popular songs in many different genres, and from time to time he would try out an original song.

Young people on their way to the Avon Theater stayed outside as long as they could to hear Justin play, and some took videos of him and posted them on YouTube. One girl even gave him her number on a note she dropped in his guitar case. When Justin told Ryan and Chaz about that, they were impressed. At thirteen Justin was interested in dating, and his music was apparently a great way to meet girls.

Viral Videos

One day, while Justin was looking for a busking video that someone had posted for him on YouTube, he checked on the videos his mother had posted of his Stratford Star performance. To his surprise, they had gotten hundreds of hits. It seemed that word was spreading about him on the Internet, and Justin had fans. According to the comments, girls thought he was cute, and older people were amazed that such a young boy could sing and play so well. He was even earning YouTube honors, which are awarded to videos that rate highest on a given day.

By 2007 YouTube had become extremely popular with young people, and many of them used the video-sharing site to discover new music. Though Justin did not realize it, he was getting exposure on a marketing platform that the music industry had not yet discovered—one that was reaching millions of young people who were sharing videos with their friends. Justin and his mother began videotaping Justin performing in his room. His fan base grew, and his videos began going viral—meaning that the number of people watching his videos was growing exponentially

Justin's fan base began to grow as videos of him busking hit YouTube. These videos prompted interest from the entertainment industry.

as fans forwarded them to their friends. By the end of that summer, some of his videos had accumulated almost one hundred thousand hits.

The entertainment industry was also taking notice. Mallette began to receive calls from agents wanting to represent Justin. She also heard from television shows interested in having him appear. While Justin was excited by this, Mallette was suspicious. She doubted the calls were legitimate, and even if they were, she did not want her son working in the music industry, which she believed exploited young talent. Many promising young artists had ruined their careers by becoming hooked on drugs and alcohol, and Mallette had personal experience with the dangers of the partying lifestyle. It also seemed unlikely that her son, who had never had a formal lesson, could become successful. It was not that she doubted Justin's talent or did not want success for him—she just knew how long the odds were of making it in the music industry.

The Call of a Lifetime

One of the callers was especially persistent. Scooter Braun, a young, independent music promoter from Atlanta, had seen Justin on YouTube and recognized his potential. Mallette was not even answering her phone by this time, so Braun called Justin's relatives, as well as his school, hoping to get a message to Mallette. She finally called Braun back—from an anonymous number. After a two-hour conversation, Braun convinced her that he was legitimate. He wanted to fly Justin and Mallette to Atlanta to discuss Justin's career. "I just want to say I see something really special in your son," he told Mallette. "I think I can help him. ... The biggest thing you've got to know about me, is that I want to make sure your son never has any 'what ifs.'"[28]

Braun had an impressive list of credentials: He was a former executive at the music label So So Def, and he had just signed the rapper Asher Roth. Mallette discussed her values and morals with him, and she decided to trust him. Mallette and Justin put their trip to Disney World on hold and flew to Atlanta.

Independent music promoter Scooter Braun convinced Justin's mom Pattie to let him bring Justin to the attention of those in the music industry. Justin's relationship with Scooter was very successful.

The trip went well. It was Justin's first time on an airplane, and he was excited. Braun picked them up at the airport in a purple Mercedes and took them to Jermaine Dupri's recording studio. Dupri is a successful rapper and record producer who has worked with artists like Mariah Carey and Boyz II Men. Braun wanted Dupri and Justin to get to know each other. One thing that Braun was very clear about was that he did not want Justin to sing yet. He wanted to create a buzz around Justin, so that when he finally did sing, industry executives would give Justin their full attention.

But Justin had a hard time keeping quiet, especially when he spotted one of his idols, the rhythm-and-blues (R&B) singer Usher Raymond, outside the studio. Before Braun could stop him, Justin ran up to Usher (who only uses his first name professionally) and

Scooter Braun

Talent manager Scott Samuel "Scooter" Braun was born on June 18, 1981. Like his most famous artist, Justin Bieber, Braun made his mark in the entertainment industry early. In middle school he entered a documentary contest with a short film about the Holocaust called *The Hungarian Conflict*. The film placed third and came to the attention of Steven Spielberg, who sent it to the U.S. Holocaust Memorial Museum, where it can still be seen today.

Braun went to Emory University, where he found he had a knack for throwing parties. As a sophomore he decided to form his own party-promotion business. His parties began to draw celebrities like Britney Spears and Ludacris, which in turn caught the attention of Jermaine Dupri, head of So So Def Recordings. Dupri offered Braun a job, and by the time Braun was twenty, Dupri appointed him executive director of the label. Braun continued to produce celebrity parties and attend college until his junior year, when he dropped out to pursue his career full-time.

Braun left So So Def to form his own music label, School Boy Records, which has a special business arrangement with Universal Music Group. When he first met Justin Bieber, he had just signed rapper Asher Roth to School Boy. To handle Bieber's career, he formed a second label with rap star Usher called the Raymond-Braun Media Group.

asked if he could sing for him. Usher, who thought Justin was one of Braun's relatives, politely turned him down. Later, up in the studio, and despite Braun's warnings, Justin started rapping and singing for Dupri. Braun was discovering how enthusiastic—and fearless—Justin could be. When he met his music idols, instead of being nervous, Justin wanted to sing their own songs to them.

Justin, Mallette, and Braun left the studio and spent the rest of the trip getting to know each other. They had dinner with

Braun's parents, and Mallette was impressed. Justin remembers, "Mom decided this Scooter guy in the purple pimpmobile was okay after all. He had a strong Jewish faith. His family was loving, rock solid and successful. Sure he was young, but he was polite and super-motivated. He knew a lot about the business. And he believed in me."[29] Mallette decided to trust Scooter and let him represent her son.

An Innovative Plan

Braun's plan was to use Justin's growing fan base on YouTube to catch the interest of a major recording label. At the time, the music industry rarely took a chance on unknown artists. Big music companies wanted to sign artists who could show they already had fans. Braun instructed Mallette and Justin to continue posting videos and growing his fan base. Braun told the *New York Times*, "I said: 'Justin, sing like there's no one in the room. But let's not use expensive cameras.' We'll give it to kids, let them do the work, so that they feel like it's theirs."[30]

When Justin and Mallette returned to Stratford, they did just that. Justin recorded songs that he and Braun thought would show off his talents and uploaded them to YouTube. He was still gaining fans at an exponential rate, and by February his new videos were receiving 1 million hits. His videos looked homemade, which was exactly what Braun wanted. Part of the reason that Justin was becoming so popular was because he was doing what many teens were doing: making home movies and posting them on the Internet. Also, through the comment feature on YouTube, fans could communicate with Justin directly. To his fans, Justin was just like them.

"A Fellow Astronaut"

The music industry was not impressed. No one was interested in a young singer who had never performed professionally. Justin remembers, "Scooter kept trying to tell people, 'This kid already has a huge fan base. They're out there. If we give them

Justin's music career began with a partnership with Usher (left), who led the young performer to the record producer who gave Justin his first record deal.

the records, they'll do the rest.' But that had never been done in the music business. Everyone understood the concept of a viral video, but no one had ever used that to successfully launch a major act."[31]

Braun had his own label, School Boy Records, but he needed the backing of a major recording group that had the resources to launch Justin's career. After months of trying to interest a major label, Braun decided he needed to partner with a successful artist, someone who could vouch for Justin with label executives. He decided to approach two former child stars who had a good reputation in the industry, Usher and Justin Timberlake. Usher had made his start on the television show *Star Search*, and Timberlake had been on the Disney Channel's *Mickey Mouse Club* before joining the boy band 'N Sync. After watching the YouTube videos and meeting Justin Bieber, both were interested. Now Justin had to decide which of these artists could best help manage his career.

He chose Usher, in large part because he believed Usher knew exactly what he would be going through if he made it big. "If you're an astronaut going to the moon," Usher explained to Justin, "there's not a whole lot of people in the world with whom you can share the experience. Well, I'm a fellow astronaut. I've been to the moon. I can talk you up and get you back down safely."[32] Usher was a young teenager when he signed with record executive L.A. Reid after competing on *Star Search*, which was similar to *American Idol*. Mallette was impressed by Usher's willingness to help Justin navigate what was ahead, and she approved of the decision. Braun and Usher formed a legal partnership so that they could jointly manage Justin's career.

Usher decided that the record producer who had given him his start, L.A. Reid, was the perfect person to approach. Reid had a long, solid history of making artists into stars, having helped singers like Mariah Carey and Rihanna achieve multiplatinum record sales. Reid was the chief executive officer of the record label Island Def Jam Music Group, and he agreed to meet Justin.

Usher

Usher Terry Raymond IV was born October 14, 1978. At age thirteen he was a contestant on *Star Search*, a talent competition similar to *American Idol*. His performance caught the attention of L.A. Reid, the cofounder of LaFace Records. Reid signed the teenager and arranged for Sean "P. Diddy" Combs

Usher performs at a concert in South Africa in 2012. The popular performer has also worked as an actor and is an entrepreneur.

to produce several of the tracks on Usher's first album, which peaked at twenty-five on the *Billboard* Top R&B/Hip-Hop Albums chart. Usher went on to record six more albums and has sold more than 65 million records worldwide, becoming one of the best-selling artists in music history. He has been nominated for well over one hundred awards and has won dozens, including winning seven Grammy Awards.

Usher is also an actor, entrepreneur, and philanthropist. As a teenager he had a recurring role on the television show *Moesha* and later appeared in films such as *The Faculty*, *She's All That*, and *Light It Up*. He owns several restaurants and is part owner of the Cleveland Cavaliers basketball team. In 1999 he founded the New Look Foundation, which helps young people in trouble see alternative futures. In 2006 New Look began an effort to rebuild New Orleans after Hurricane Katrina. Usher was also part of *A Concert for Hurricane Relief*, a telethon that supported Hurricane Katrina relief efforts and featured live performances from artists across the country.

Justin was nervous, but he performed well, singing and playing guitar for Reid in his office in New York. Finally, in April 2008, nearly a year after Braun first contacted him, Justin got a record contract with Island Def Jam. He had just turned fourteen.

It took another six months for Justin and his mother to arrange to move from Canada to the United States. In the meantime Justin continued to write songs, practice performing in front of the Avon Theater, and upload videos to YouTube. Once they finally moved to Atlanta, Braun set Justin up with his vocal coach, Jan Smith, who had helped Usher through the vocal changes that happen to boys in puberty. Justin also began studying with a tutor from the School of Young Performers. Because he was only fourteen, he had to study a certain number of hours each day, and there were restrictions to how many hours he was allowed to work.

The Power of Twitter

When everyone was convinced that Justin's voice was ready, he began recording singles for his first album. Braun had identified a dozen songs that fit Justin's style and showed off his vocal skills. Justin wrote some of the songs himself, and on others he collaborated on with a team of songwriters that included Usher. Braun and Reid planned to bring Justin into the public eye in a big way, saturating the market with two albums released four months apart. Before the album's debut, they would release a few of the songs as singles to create interest in the upcoming album. Since Justin already had a strong Internet following, Braun wanted to use the Internet as the primary medium to intensify the buzz about Justin.

They filmed a video of his song "One Time" and arranged for iTunes to heavily advertise its release, which was planned for two weeks after the single appeared on the site. Braun hoped to create anticipation about the video with the advertizing blitz. But things did not go as planned. The video was mistakenly released two weeks early, on a Friday night, with no promotion whatsoever. Braun was furious. There was no way to find the video on the site unless you specifically searched for it, and since no one even

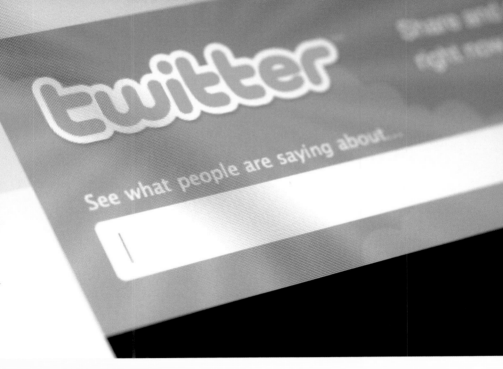

Social networking sites like Twitter were very successful in building Justin's fan base. Justin tweeted about songs, videos, and performances, and fans eagerly responded.

knew it existed, the buzz Braun hoped to create was not going to happen.

Braun had an idea. Justin had just started a Facebook and Twitter account, and he and Braun decided to use the social networking sites to create the buzz they needed. "I got on there and started tweeting my brains out," Justin remembers. "I followed all my followers and friended their friends. I replied and retweeted and commented and tweeted back and forth as the conversation got bigger and bigger."[33] Because Justin had already created a fan base on YouTube, he was able to reach those fans directly on Twitter. Fans flocked to iTunes to buy the single and download the video. By the following Tuesday, "One Time" was the second-most popular video on iTunes.

Once again, the strategy worked: Justin reached out to fans directly using social networking, and they responded in large numbers. Finally, Justin's label—as well as the music industry—began to understand the power of connecting with fans personally and mobilizing them at the grassroots level.

"Hand-to-Hand Combat"

That summer Justin released four singles to create interest in his album, *My World*, which was scheduled for release in November 2009. All four were extremely popular on iTunes, but they were not getting any airplay on the radio. The problem was that Justin was too young. Radio stations almost always target adult listeners, and music that appeals to tweens and young teenagers rarely gets played, regardless of how popular it is on iTunes. Braun decided that the only way to get airplay for Justin's music was to visit the radio stations personally. "Hand-to-hand combat is what we did," Braun explained. "He went to every single one.

Justin performs to promote his first album My World in 2009. His popularity quickly became news, being dubbed "Bieber Fever."

If you weren't playing his record, he still went, and he'd play his guitar for you acoustic, and he'd sing on the spot any request, and he won people over. There's not a DJ [disc jockey] who can say they have not met Justin Bieber."[34] Justin also appeared at any venue that would have him. He played shopping malls, water parks, and high schools. He used Twitter to promote his appearances, reaching out personally to his fans and asking them to support him.

The strategy worked. At first, forty or fifty girls showed up at Justin's appearances. But as fans spread the word, retweeting Justin's Twitter posts to their followers, girls began showing up in greater and greater numbers, hoping to catch a glimpse of the young singer. Stations that previously had no interest in playing a fifteen-year-old's music were confronted with hundreds of fans outside their doors, clamoring for Justin. DJs began playing his songs, and all four singles rose to within the top forty of the *Billboard* Hot 100 chart.

By the second half of 2009, Justin was being invited all over the world to perform and promote his upcoming album. *My World* was released in November, and by then more fans were showing up than some venues could safely handle. One appearance at a Long Island shopping mall was canceled because too many people were inside and there was not adequate crowd control. Authorities requested that Bieber's team send out a tweet canceling the event, but it was too late to prevent several fans from being injured by the crowd. Both Braun and an executive from the record label were arrested on charges that included endangerment. By this time Justin was on the radar of the mainstream media, and the incident got a lot of attention. The very fact of Justin's popularity became news, and the media dubbed this "Bieber Fever," comparing it to Beatlemania of the 1960s.

My World was a huge success. Justin's record label predicted that, based on his unusual niche—a young, white R&B singer who had gained a following through social media—the album would sell about sixty thousand copies in the first five weeks. They had not taken into account the power of his fans to network, spreading the word about Justin in a grassroots effort to personally help the young singer succeed. In five weeks *My World* sold nearly nine hundred thousand copies in the United States, almost fifteen times the predicted amount.

They Did It Their Way

Braun's innovative strategy for promoting Justin had been a success. "Everything about the way *My World* was released turned the old way of thinking inside out," Justin explains. "A skinny white kid on a record with rappers with serious street cred. A teen fan favorite with no TV show. ... I'm sure me and the team would love to take credit for this, but the truth of it is that it all happened because of [my fans]. We are good, but we aren't that good."[35] Before Justin's success, the music industry did not appreciate the potential of social media sites like YouTube and networking sites like Facebook and Twitter as ways to reach young music fans. But after the breakout success of *My World*, no one could deny the power of social networking. In fact, Justin's success has spawned an entire industry of independent promoters who specialize in bringing rising Internet stars to major labels, and the labels themselves now search for talent on YouTube instead of in local clubs. Thousands of young singers and musicians have started their own YouTube followings, and some are making a comfortable living without the help of a label.

Chapter 4

The Image of a Superstar

In the modern entertainment industry, an artist's image is usually treated as a brand. Marketers try to associate an artist's name with an emotional response: Lady Gaga's brand is about nonconformity and independence, while Bruce Springsteen's brand evokes working-class strength and rebelliousness. The characteristics that make up an artist's brand usually come directly from his or her own personality and vision, which is why the industry sometimes values star quality over talent.

After the success of *My World*, Justin Bieber was on his way to being a pop star. He had millions of devoted young fans, who saw him as both a role model and a regular kid. However, many adults assumed Justin was just another squeaky-clean child star created by the record label's marketing machine. Some called his music bubblegum pop, a term that refers to catchy, formulaic music that is produced by the industry in an assembly line process and contrived to appeal specifically to tweens and young teens. The *New York Times* described his music as "a low-calorie confection of R & B pop tunes swirled through with head-bobbing urgency and hip-hop grace notes."[36] The mainstream media was not taking Justin seriously as a musician, which only supported the perception that he was simply a creation of the entertainment industry.

The Bigger You Are, the Harder You Fall

Despite the criticism he faced from adults, Justin began getting invitations to play all over the world. He opened for Taylor Swift in London's Wembley Arena before an audience of twelve thousand people—his largest audience to date. During that performance he broke his foot onstage, right in the middle

Justin performs in London in 2010. He opened for Taylor Swift during a concert in the city that year, followed by several other important performances.

of a song, but he hid the injury from the audience and sang through the pain. He refused to let the injury interfere with his momentum, and a few weeks later he played for President Barack Obama and his family at the annual Christmas in Washington concert. On December 31 he performed live on *Dick Clark's New Year's Rockin' Eve with Ryan Seacrest*, and in February 2010 he released his second album, *My World 2.0*, which debuted at number one on the *Billboard* 200 chart. A few months later he was the musical guest on *Saturday Night Live* and was interviewed on *Oprah*. These televised appearances gave Justin a lot of exposure among adults who did not necessarily know his music and introduced him to millions of new teen and tween fans.

But despite these successes, many adults formed a negative opinion about Justin. The more media coverage he received, the

A Dreamy Christmas Elf

In 2010 Justin Bieber appeared as the musical guest on *Saturday Night Live*. Along with performing his singles "Baby" and "U Smile," he also acted in two skits with that week's host, Tina Fey. It was one of Justin's first stints as an actor. In one of the skits, he played a student named Jason who flirts with his teacher to improve his grades. Fey plays the teacher, and in the skit she finds herself unnaturally attracted to the boy, whom she describes as "a dreamy Christmas elf." The routine is a wry commentary on older women who are devoted Justin Bieber fans and profess to be in love with the teenager, something that both Justin and his mother, Patti Mallette, find disturbing. Justin also acted in *Saturday Night Live*'s "100th Digital Short" and will host the show in 2012.

Tina Fey. *Saturday Night Live*. NBC, April 10, 2010.

more he seemed to remind adults about aspects of young people they find shallow, even annoying. One reporter expressed this attitude when writing about a poll that predicted Justin's fame would be short-lived. "Justin Bieber won't be around much longer to torture us with his floppy hair, faux-hip-hoppy-ness, gross-out teenage PDA [public display of affection], and Twitter trending,"[37] she wrote. Justin was dating the pop star Selena Gomez, and pictures of the two teenagers (dubbed "Jelena" by the press) kissing and holding hands appeared regularly in tabloids and entertainment magazines.

The media—and the public—was quick to mock Justin, even for minor mistakes. In a New Zealand interview, Justin had difficulty understanding the interviewer's accent, and his confusion was misunderstood to mean that he had never heard of the country Germany. That incident was widely reported in the blogosphere, and a video clip of the interview quickly went viral. Mainstream magazine articles were often written in a tone that was at once mocking and sympathetic, mirroring the public perception that Justin was just a product of the music industry and was being used for financial gain. A reporter for the *Atlantic* writes, "The kid is teenybop-perfect, eagerly suspending his charm-particles in the requisite solution of pure nonentity. He smiles, he thanks, he praises; he displays a persona from which every hint of psychology has been combed out."[38] The writer implies that Justin has been coached so thoroughly by his handlers that any remnants of his true personality have been eliminated.

As his popularity with the youth market grew and more adults became aware of him, the negative backlash to his success continued. Websites making fun of the star were beginning to rival the number of fan sites devoted to him, and one Bieber detractor even developed a computer application that blocked any mention of Justin Bieber from web-browsing sessions. Whether these detractors were suspicious that the star's image was manufactured or were simply annoyed by the media's fascination with the young star, one thing was clear: Justin was becoming a popular person to hate.

Not Just a Pretty Face

Even though many people thought negatively of Justin, his management team did not want to try to radically change his image or make him something that he was not. Justin really was squeaky-clean: He was a Christian who valued his family and was staunchly against drug use. He was a good kid, and his mother wanted him to stay that way. She and Braun had worked hard to make sure that he was surrounded by good influences and that he was treated like a teenager, not like a superstar. "I don't care about the money," Mallette said. "I don't care about the fame. I care about him being a good person."[39]

As Justin prepared for his seventeen-month *My World* tour, he struggled with how to let the world know the real Justin Bieber. His team did not want to contradict the good-kid persona that had made him a strong role model for his fans, many of whom were still young enough to need their parents' approval for the music they listened to. Instead, they would expand that image and show the world the talented, intelligent, playful side of Justin. One reason teenagers liked him was because he was a natural leader, self-confident and funny, and was not above making fun of himself. It was time to show everyone that side.

Flooding the Media

Scooter Braun arranged for HarperCollins to publish Justin's memoir, *First Step 2 Forever: My Story*. Written by Justin (or, as is common, a ghostwriter working with Justin), it is a first-person account of his rise to fame, interspersed with stories of the days before his first performance on the *My World* tour. The memoir is written as if Justin is speaking directly to his fans, creating the same sort of intimacy that his connections on Twitter created. It showcases Justin's moral side, but it also tweaks his good-kid image: he is a prankster, he is impatient, he is hyper—in other words, he is a typical teenager. Tales of getting in trouble with his friends at school are interspersed with dating advice that shows unusual maturity. "You don't have to work hard at pretending you

Justin published a memoir in 2010 as part of a media blitz promoting the rising artist. The book was followed by a biopic a few months later. All depicted Justin as a nice, regular kid and a positive role model.

care about a girl's feelings if you actually do care—not just about girls, but about people in general,"[40] he says.

Justin admits to hiding his talent from his schoolmates to avoid being teased, and to failing his driver's license test because he was too cocky to study. But he also talks about his love of family and his interest in charity work, inspired not only by his Christian beliefs but also by his hero, Michael Jackson. "If I can do just one-tenth of the good he [Jackson] did for others, I can really make a difference in this world," he says. "That's what this is all about."[41] The memoir gives a well-rounded picture of Justin and dispels misperceptions that his image was manufactured by the music industry.

Braun also partnered with director John Chu to create a 3-D video documentary chronicling Justin's rise to fame. Interspersed with footage from his *My World* tour, this biopic follows a format similar to the memoir—behind-the-scenes glimpses of Justin on tour woven together with home movies and interviews with friends and family. Justin apes for the camera, pulls pranks on his staff, and grumbles about not being able to eat McDonald's food before a show. But it also shows him saying grace before eating pizza with his friends, bringing one of his youngest fans onstage with him to share a song, and worrying about his voice failing before his concert at Madison Square Garden.

The memoir was released in November 2010 and the biopic in February 2011. Braun was saturating the market with his artist. By early 2011 Justin had two albums on the charts, he was in the middle of a world tour, he was on television, his memoir was a *New York Times* best seller, and his movie had earned nearly $100 million worldwide.

Taken together, his memoir and biopic portray Justin as a kid that most parents would want their children to look up to. Some reviewers speculated that the book and the movie were being marketed not to teens and tweens but to their parents. Justin himself was aware of the importance of having parents on board. "I hope your parents like me,"[42] he deadpans to the camera in a spoof of himself on the website Funny or Die. Instead of changing Justin's good-kid image so that he would appeal to a broader audience, Braun had reinforced the star's moral side while also showing him to be an independent thinker, a driven and talented performer, and a "regular" kid who pranks his friends and occasionally gets into trouble.

Controversies

Even with this positive portrayal, Justin was still a magnet for controversy. In an interview with *Rolling Stone* before the premiere of his biopic, comments he made about rape and abortion sparked a controversy. The interviewer writes:

> He's definitely against abortion, too. "I really don't believe in abortion. I think [an embryo] is a human. It's like killing a baby." Even in the case of rape? "Um," he says. "Well, I think that's just really sad, but everything happens for a reason. I don't know how that would be a reason." He looks confused. "I guess I haven't been in that position, so I wouldn't be able to judge that."[43]

Detractors interpreted his comments to mean that Bieber believed that if a woman was raped, it was part of God's plan. The misunderstanding happened because part of his comment, "I don't know how that would be a reason," was omitted from the Internet version of the article.

Justin never clarified his comments, and his words seemed to reflect a simplistic understanding of the issues that is typical of teenagers. Talk shows all over the country began discussing the issue, some criticizing Justin's views and some criticizing the magazine for asking inappropriate questions. One host of the television show *The View* commented that Bieber's statement was "really insulting to people who have been raped or victims of incest."[44] However, the *Rolling Stone* interviewer, Vanessa Grigoriadis, claimed that the media was misinterpreting Bieber's responses to her questions. "I think he meant that God has a plan," she said. "Even for the most die-hard Christian, it's hard to justify rape as part of God's plan, and harder to justify rape that leads to pregnancy and abortion. I think he was wrestling with that in his answer, which I found to be solid and logical. I think it is being widely misunderstood. He did not say that rape was part of God's plan."[45]

Negative public perception continued to follow Justin. He was booed by the crowd at a New York Knicks game when a shot of him sitting in the stands was projected on the arena's big screen. He was criticized for flipping his middle finger at members of the press and for swearing at a fan who harassed him at Disney World. The French media reported that Justin ran from fans at an airport, which was particularly disturbing to him because he had actually been running from paparazzi (freelance photographers). A *Forbes* article titled "Justin Bieber's Days Are Numbered" cited a poll done on Sodahead.com that found that 76 percent of Justin's fans did not expect him to be popular in ten years.

Baby Mama Drama

The biggest controversy occurred in October 2011, when a woman named Mariah Yeater filed a paternity suit against Justin, claiming that she had just given birth to his baby. Yeater said that nine months before, she and Justin had sex in the bathroom after one of his shows. The story made headlines for weeks, in part because the accusation contradicted Justin's image in such a shocking way. Previously, Justin had claimed that he was a virgin and would not have sex unless he was in love. Though he denied Yeater's paternity claims again and again, the story headlined the news for weeks.

It was not until Justin appeared on the entertainment television show *Extra* with Braun that the tide of popular opinion began to turn. Again, Justin flatly denied the claim. He had never met Yeater, and he planned to take a paternity test to set the record straight. Justin explained that he was taking the paternity test voluntarily so that anyone else tempted to make false claims against him would realize that he would fight the accusations. "It could happen again," Justin said. "We don't want to make it seem like it's okay for everyone else."[46] Braun went on to say that legal action would be taken against Yeater. "He's trying to be a role model, and

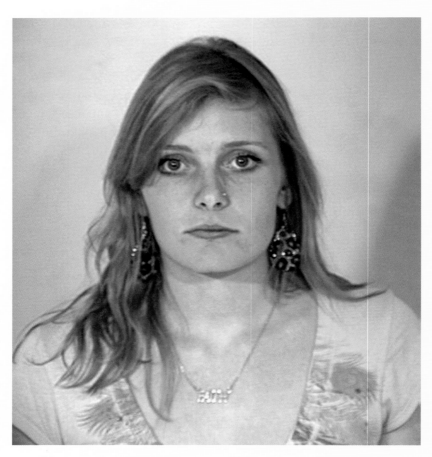

Justin's image and career underwent controversy when Mariah Yeater claimed that Justin was the father of her baby. Justin fought the allegations, which threatened to damage his reputation.

you're not going to come in and just slander him and feel like you can walk away. ... If you go after someone, there's going to be consequences to your actions when you make something up and you blatantly lie."[47] Soon after, Yeater dropped the suit.

Justin's reaction to Yeater's accusations did more to change public opinion than the efforts of his marketing team. Some

Jelena

Much to the dismay of lovesick Justin Bieber fans, in early 2010 Selena Gomez announced that she and Justin were dating. The two had been best friends for some time, but they had kept their romantic relationship private for about three months, in part to avoid the backlash that Selena would face from the Beliebers, who had been known to threaten any woman Justin expressed a romantic interest in.

Though Selena initially had a hard time dealing with angry Bieber fans, who were heartbroken that Justin was unavailable, she and Justin quickly became media favorites, and pic-

Selena Gomez and Justin Bieber began dating in early 2010. When word got out that the two were a couple, it angered many lovesick Bieber fans, but the two quickly became a media favorite.

tures of the two of them holding hands and kissing in public soon filled the tabloids. As of mid-2012, the couple was still going strong.

Selena Gomez is a pop singer and actress who got her start on the children's television show *Barney & Friends* when she was seven years old. She later caught the interest of the Disney Chanel and appeared in several Disney programs until landing a lead role in the series *Wizards of Waverly Place*. In 2009 she formed the teen pop band Selena Gomez & the Scene, which went on to sell more than 3 million albums worldwide. Recently, she took a hiatus from singing to concentrate on her acting career.

changed their opinion of him, seeing him now as a serious and composed young man who had been used by an unscrupulous woman. Stories in the media began to focus less on public gaffes and possible controversies and more on Justin's transition to adulthood.

Moving On

Justin tried not to let the controversies interfere with his career. He continued performing and making public appearances. He licensed a celebrity perfume to be marketed to fourteen- to eighteen-year-old girls and donated all proceeds to charity. He followed his second album, *My World 2.0*, with an acoustic compilation album (*My World Acoustic*) in 2010, and then released two more compilation albums in 2011. *Never Say Never: The Remixes*, featured a new song from the soundtrack of *The Karate Kid* (2010), recorded with the film's star, Jaden Smith. *Under the Mistletoe* featured Christmas standards and collaborations

With his next album, Believe, Justin wanted to show a more mature side of himself.

with artists such as Boyz II Men and Mariah Carey. Both albums debuted at number one on the *Billboard* charts, making Justin the first solo artist to have three number one albums before the age of eighteen.

In 2011 Justin began expressing a desire to be viewed as a more mature artist. He hoped his upcoming album, *Believe*, would show people that he could do more than sing sugary pop songs about teen romance. He was featured on the cover of *Complex* magazine, where he appeared with his shirt torn and his face bloodied under the headline "Justin Bieber: Second Round KO." The feature article discusses the way Justin's image is changing. Braun says, "As adults we think about that transition when you started living young manhood. He'll represent that. I don't think there's anything that needs to be done. The one thing I tell him all the time is, 'Don't be in such a rush to appease the adult audience and try to be a grown-up. Just be eighteen—and people will relate to that.'"[48]

Here to Stay

Despite a great deal of negative media attention, Justin Bieber has remained one of the biggest celebrities in the world. Between 2009 and 2012 he sold more than 15 million albums. He was named the third-most powerful celebrity in the world by *Forbes* magazine two years in a row (behind Jennifer Lopez and Oprah Winfrey), and was featured on the magazine's cover in 2012. He is estimated to have earned over $108 million in 2010 and 2011. By 2012 he had 28 million Twitter followers and 43 million Facebook fans. His image has morphed from squeaky-clean child pop star to talented and mature adult firmly in control of his career. And while the "haters" still abound, Justin's vast and loyal fan base make it likely he will be a force in the music industry for years to come.

Chapter 5

The Power of the Beliebers

For as long as there has been music, there have been music fans. Fans of the Grateful Dead call themselves "Deadheads"; Lady Gaga fans dub themselves "Little Monsters." Justin Bieber fans also have a catchy nickname: "Beliebers." The term is more than just a pun on Justin's last name; it reflects his fans' perception that his fame is due to their unwavering belief in both his talent and his character. The Beliebers have a sense of ownership when it

A mass of Justin Bieber's fans gather in Madrid, Spain, in 2012. Justin's fans are very devoted and gained the nickname "Beliebers."

comes to Justin Bieber. In a typical tweet to his fans, Justin wrote, "we came up from the bottom TOGETHER. every step we were doubted. I doubted … but you were always there."[49]

No artist can be successful without fans, but Justin Bieber's unique fan base has influenced his career more than his own marketing team. The Beliebers have not only created a superstar; they have completely changed the way music labels market their artists.

The Way It Used to Be

Before the advent of YouTube and other social media sites, the only way a recording artist could find a large audience was to get help from a recording label. There were only a few ways to get the attention of a label: Artists could perform in venues frequented by music promoters, they could get the support of a successful artist, or they could send a demo—a sample of their music either recorded on personal equipment or in a local studio—directly to the label. In the past many artists spent their days promoting their music and their nights performing, all in the hope of one day being discovered. The process was slow and costly, and it often took years.

If an artist was offered a record contract, it did not necessarily mean that he or she would find an audience. Record labels rarely put much money into marketing a new artist unless they believe the artist has the potential to be a breakout success. Labels have dropped many talented singers and musicians not because they lacked talent, but because not enough effort was put into finding an audience for their music. It was a no-win situation: A label was rarely interested in an artist who did not have a fan base, but it was difficult to develop a fan base without the help of a label.

A New Kind of Fan

All of this changed in the digital age. Instead of paying for costly studio rentals and going through the time-consuming process of mailing out demo recordings, today musicians can reach fans directly on the Internet. With the advent of new technologies, they can record themselves cheaply and post their performances

Fans have been very important to building Justin Bieber's career. Some earlier artists, such as Elvis Presley, also owed their early success to young fans.

online for free. Once their material is on a media-sharing site like YouTube, it is immediately available to millions of people, and fans can then use social networking sites like Facebook to share the video with their friends. The British singer Susan Boyle, for example, became a worldwide sensation after her audition for the television show *Britain's Got Talent* went viral on YouTube.

Social news sites like Digg and Reddit, which rank user-submitted links by popularity, are also a boon to musicians. These sites make popular links even more popular by featuring them to their millions of subscribers. Singer-songwriter Jonathan Coulton gained a strong fan following when his folksy cover of Sir Mix-a-Lot's rap song "Baby Got Back" became popular on Slashdot, a social news website. In the digital age, artists are able to record, market, and even sell their music without the help of a record label.

By the time Justin Bieber posted his first video on YouTube, the music industry's most coveted demographic—teenagers and tweens—were using the Internet as their primary method of discovering and sharing new music. These are the fans who have always created pop superstars; Frank Sinatra, Elvis Presley, and the Beatles all owed their initial success to their popularity with young fans. As one radio personality remarked, "As long as the girls are screaming, somebody's selling records."[50]

Who Are the Beliebers?

The typical Justin Bieber fan is under eighteen, female, and claims to be deeply in love with the young star. Many adults do not understand Justin's appeal, but it is not surprising—a youthful appearance and soft, slightly feminine features have always been popular with young girls, perhaps because at a time in their lives when they are just discovering their own sexuality, they are less threatened by youthful, boyish looks. Justin resembles a young Paul McCartney, who also had full cheeks and a mop-top haircut at the height of Beatlemania in the 1960s.

Young girls also relate to Justin's music, which is mainly about courtship and falling in love, a common preoccupation of that age group. When asked why she considered herself a Belieber, one fan explained, "It was because of his talent, and because he's so cute. Also, I think it's nice for a girl to hear songs from a boy's perspective; it's like he's singing just to me." She went on to explain why she and her friends scream so hysterically over the star—the phenomenon the media has dubbed "Bieber Fever" and compares to Beatlemania: "Because you're watching the videos and the pictures online and listening to the music, then, finally, you see him. And you just can't help it—you're screaming at the top of your lungs."[51]

What sets the Beliebers apart from female fans of the past is their sense of connection to the artist. Most Beliebers profess to have known Justin since the beginning, and they believe—quite rightly—that they are responsible for his success. As Justin's tour manager, Allison Kaye, comments, "Justin has the most loyal fans on the planet."[52] His manager, Scooter Braun, realized this early on, which was why he encouraged Justin to make his own videos.

Justin Bieber reaches out to fans during a concert. Justin's devoted fans, called Beliebers, are mostly young girls attracted to his talent and good looks.

The music was free, and the homemade videos seemed to have no connection to the music industry, which made fans feel as if they had discovered Justin themselves.

That loyalty has placed Justin in a unique position. Since he communicates with his fans directly on Twitter, he can influence them without any help from his label. In the past if an artist did not like a marketing strategy, he or she had little recourse. But Justin's fans have developed their own communication network and are able to affect record and concert sales without any help from the

Intimate Concerts

Justin Bieber's fans love the way the singer engages them on what they perceive to be a personal level. For this reason they flock to concerts, wait in line for hours to see him, and nearly fall to pieces when they finally get that chance. In a *Time* magazine article, reporter Claire Suddath described the scene at a typical Justin Bieber concert:

> Bieber gave a small concert at New York's Highline Ballroom for several hundred teenage girls, many of whom had waited for up to five hours to win tickets through a local radio station. The girls wore Bieber T-shirts, carried Bieber CDs and had Bieber backgrounds on their cell phones. "He's so sweet. He's not like every other guy who is just like, 'Ugh, whatever,'" says Alicia Isaacson, 13, from Long Island. ... Every few seconds, a shrill cry of "Justin!" erupted from somewhere in the crowd. Security guards handed out water bottles and escorted those who felt faint or overwhelmed outside.

Claire Suddath. "How the Internet Made Justin Bieber a Star." *Time*, May 17, 2010. www .time.com/time/magazine/article/0,9171,1987603,00.html.

industry. This gives Justin an enormous amount of power in business dealings with this label and promoters. It has been speculated that if Justin wanted to fill an arena, he could do so without any promotional effort from his marketing team whatsoever.

True Devotion

Before Justin began dating the pop star Selena Gomez, his singleness was hugely appealing to his fans. Like many teen idols before him, when Justin sings about his own longing for true love, a girl imagines that this boy will choose her. Some girls sport T-shirts that read "The Future Mrs. Bieber" and insist that they will marry the star one day. They beg him to notice them on Twitter, and many have been scammed by websites claiming to have the secret to getting Justin to follow their Twitter feed. Fans who are lucky enough to have Justin as a Twitter follower proudly announce the date he began to follow them in their profile.

Justin encourages this devotion by paying surprise visits to fans, giving away free tickets, and serenading an audience member onstage with his song "One Less Lonely Girl." His fans range in age from toddlers to grandmothers, and Justin pays special attention to his youngest fans. When a video of a three-year-old girl named Cody, who was weeping because she wanted to see "Justin Beaver," went viral on YouTube, Justin visited her at her home.

He is not as charitable toward his older female fans, however, and his mother finds the attention he often receives from grown women inappropriate and disturbing. "The mothers are the worst,"[53] she said to a reporter after a mom pushed a cell phone in her son's face.

Fans Mobilized

The Beliebers have a huge Internet presence. Fans from all over the world have created hundreds of websites devoted to Justin. While fan clubs are nothing new—teen idols of the 1970s like David Cassidy and Donny Osmond had both official and unofficial fan clubs—Bieber fans are the first major fan base with the ability to communicate as a group online. They stay connected through networking sites like Twitter and Facebook, which allow them to share information instantly. Justin taps into this network and uses it both for promotion and to keep his fans happy. He informs them about upcoming shows and "secret" free performances. The power of this type of promotion was made clear in May 2012, when Justin tweeted about a free fan concert at a venue in Oslo, Norway. Fan turnout was so great that the Red Cross was called in to distribute water to the thousands of dehydrated girls who packed the streets, and the government contemplated declaring a state of emergency. A music label might have taken several weeks and millions of dollars to organize such an event, but Justin was able to do it with a single tweet typed into his smartphone.

The power of the Beliebers comes from their ability to mobilize. They often organize campaigns (which they call "Bieber Blasts") to completely buy out a music store's inventory of a new Justin Bieber CD in an effort to push the album to number one on the first day of release. Since Justin's first video appeared on iTunes, Bieber fans have worked together to make each new video the most downloaded song on the site. Beliebers also launched a campaign in 2011 to make Justin Bieber the most followed person on Twitter, an honor that as of June 2012 was held by Lady Gaga. While the "Unfollow Lady Gaga" campaign was not successful and drew a lot of criticism from Gaga's "Little Monsters," it was partially responsible for raising Justin's Twitter numbers, which topped 28 million as of September 2012.

Beliebers also staunchly defend Justin's career when it seems threatened, sometimes with dramatic results. When the song "All Around the World" was leaked on the Internet weeks before the official release of his third album, *Believe*, many Beliebers took a vow not to listen to it so as not to dilute the excitement around the album's release. A few tweets about the incident took an ominous tone. "Whoever leaked All Around The World," tweeted a fan, "Beliebers have been known to find people's details including address and telephone number. BE SCARED."[54]

So many fans turned out for the free concert Justin announced via Twitter in 2012 that the city was unprepared and nearly declared a state of emergency.

The Dark Side of the Beliebers

Justin discovered the power he had over his fans in April 2010. A fifteen-year-old boy acquired Justin's personal number and began calling it incessantly. Fed up with the harassment, Justin countered by posting the boy's number on Twitter. By the time the boy's family changed their number a few days later, the boy had received more than twenty-six thousand angry text messages from Beliebers.

A similar thing happened in 2012, when Justin posted a message asking his fans to call him and listed a Texas number with a question mark in place of the last digit. Several Texas residents received thousands of calls from fans hoping to speak with Justin, and two of the victims of the prank have retained lawyers. It is unclear why Justin posted these numbers in the first place, and Beliebers speculate that Justin's Twitter account was hacked.

The devotion of the Beliebers sometimes turns ugly. When Justin admitted he had a crush on Kim Kardashian, Beliebers began sending her death threats on Twitter. Threats were not just reserved for Justin's romantic interests. When Justin lost to jazz singer Esperanza Spaulding for the Best New Artist Grammy Award in 2012, Spaulding's Twitter feed was flooded with angry messages, and her website was hacked and vandalized. Some Justin Bieber fans wished her dead, while others threatened to murder her. Beliebers also rushed to Justin's defense again when twenty-year-old Mariah Yeater accused him of fathering her child, harassing the woman and threatening to kill her unless she dropped the paternity suit.

Interestingly, Justin almost never criticizes his fans for their behavior. He is also not above using Twitter himself to lash out, and did so after the Mariah Yeater controversy died down. ABC News reported that on April 21, 2012,

> Bieber tweeted: "Dear mariah yeeter (sic) … we have never met … so from the heart i just wanted to say" and then he posted a link to a YouTube audio clip of the character Borat, played by comedian/actor Sacha Baron Cohen. In the clip, Borat says, mockingly: "You will never get this. You will never get this. La la la la la."[55]

After Justin admitted he had a crush on reality TV star Kim Kardashian, angry Beliebers sent her death threats.

One reason why Justin rarely criticizes his fans is that he feels genuine affection for them. Braun notes, "Justin doesn't trust many people anymore. ... But it's weird, because Justin trusts the fans. He feels like they know the real him."[56]

Austin Mahone: The Next Justin Bieber?

Sixteen-year-old Austin Mahone is a Texas-born singer who began posting videos on YouTube in 2010. He has since amassed over 1 million Internet fans, and some speculate that he could be the next Justin Bieber.

Austin is making a comfortable living from his newfound fandom. When his videos went viral in 2011, his mother quit her day job to become his full-time manager. She shoots his videos, organizes concert appearances, and sells merchandise. She also home schools Austin, though not by choice. During his first week at a new school, Austin was overwhelmed by mobs of female students. His mother was forced to take him out of school permanently.

Texas native and singer Austin Mahone has been called by some as the next Justin Bieber. Like Bieber, Mahone has built his fan base over the Internet.

Austin is still getting used to his celebrity. In Chicago he decided to tweet that he was going to take a walk in a local park, hoping that a few fans might join him. Within minutes, thousands of girls showed up, surrounding the young star and attracting the attention of the police.

Austin has released two singles on iTunes and is currently in negotiation with several recording labels.

The Power of the Crowd

The music industry has finally realized the value and power of the Internet fan. Now that technology allows videos to be created and posted on the Internet instantly, the music industry is flooding YouTube with "homemade" videos of their new artists in the hope that those videos will go viral. Rapper DeAndre Cortez Way, known as Soulja Boy, is one of a number of artists who have achieved strong fan bases using this strategy. In addition, a new industry of independent talent managers has cropped up in the wake of Justin Bieber's success. Producer and songwriter David Malloy runs a successful business coaching YouTube stars like teenage singer Austin Mahone, who has a Twitter following of nearly 1 million fans and whose YouTube videos have been viewed more than 70 million times. Mahone and thousands like him are trying to make the leap from Internet-fandom to recording artist, and Malloy hones their performance skills and introduces them to the ins and outs of the recording business. Only a few will actually get a contract with a recording label, but for most, a contract is still their end goal.

Malloy believes that the recording industry has to change if it wants to survive. He has built his success on the idea that selling CDs or downloads should no longer be the goal—especially since most music can now be downloaded for free. "The value is in the crowd," he explains to a reporter with *Texas Monthly* magazine. "Music is just a way for the fan to get to the artist."[57] Independent managers like Malloy focus on selling fans a personal experience. Income is derived not primarily from album sales but from concert tickets, festival appearances, and even one-on-one phone calls or Skype "dates" with the artist.

Still, few artists have amassed online fan bases as big as Justin Bieber's. Part of the reason for the Beliebers devotion is that they know their connection to Justin is not an artificial construct of a marketing department. Justin was one of the first to harness the power of the crowd, and his success depends entirely on his fans' faith in him. It is no coincidence that Justin titled his 2012 album *Believe*, after his fans. "I don't think of myself as powerful," he says. "If anything, my fans are powerful. It's all in their hands. If they don't buy my albums, I go away."[58]

Chapter 6

Christian Charity

Christianity has always been a part of Justin Bieber's life. "My ma has always had God around me, has always made it really apparent,"[59] Justin says, referring to how his mother helped him see how God was working in their lives. He attended an evangelical church in Stratford regularly as a child, went to Sunday school, and participated in the church's music program. Pattie Mallette never pushed her faith on her son. She waited to baptize him—a ritual that involves affirming one's faith by being immersed in water, which symbolizes the burial and resurrection of Jesus Christ—until Justin requested it himself. And when, at twelve, he decided he did not want to go to church anymore, Mallette did not force him. It is important to her that he makes his own decisions about his faith and finds his own way.

Justin was not rejecting his faith with his decision not to attend church. He considers himself deeply spiritual but not necessarily religious. He believes that going to church is not the measure of the depth of a person's faith, and that people can have a relationship with God through prayer alone. This sentiment has drawn some criticism from religious leaders, particularly since Justin is a role model to many young people. But Mallette supports it, and she does not feel that her son must practice his beliefs in the same way that she does. "He's still on his own journey," she explains. "Mine is mine, and he can't have mine. He needs his own."[60]

An Early Prophesy

Mallette believes that part of Justin's journey will be to use his fame to inspire his peers. When Justin was small, Mallette took part in what is known as a prophetic word reading, which Justin describes

In his 2011 biopic, Never Say Never, viewers learned about his Christian upbringing and importance of faith within his family.

as "sort of like fortune-telling, but from God."[61] Some Christians believe that God gives some people the gift of prophesy and that these people can channel God's word to help others understand God's plan for them. Mallette was told that her son was to be "the voice of the new generation."[62] Neither she nor Justin know exactly what this means. "It could just mean that I'm here to make music and inspire people,"[63] Justin told an interviewer. His mother thinks it means that he will influence his generation in a moral way.

What Is Evangelism?

Evangelism is the practice of spreading the Christian faith by sharing the story, or gospel, of Jesus Christ with nonbelievers. Ministries that encourage evangelism, like the church Pattie Mallette and Justin Bieber attended in their hometown, are called evangelical churches. Many Christians believe that part of their duty is to spread the word that Christ sacrificed himself to pay for our sins and that only by believing in Christ can people attain eternal life after death.

Evangelism can also include zealous or militant crusading, though most evangelists are not necessarily as zealous as television evangelists like Billy Graham or Pat Robertson. Most simply share their stories of conversion, or testify, to people who express interest. Still, the term *evangelist* has come to have a negative connotation, especially since the mid-1970s, when evangelical Christians began to flock to the Republican Party in an attempt to influence politics to support their agenda.

Evangelism takes many forms. Jehovah's Witnesses practice door-to-door evangelism. Other denominations hold evangelical events, often with entertainment. Modern Christian music is also a form of evangelism; praise bands attempt to spread a Christian message to young people through popular contemporary music.

One thing Justin is sure of is that his success is a gift from God and not necessarily something that he deserves. This perspective has helped Justin keep his ego in check and has given parents of his young fans confidence that he is a positive influence on their children.

Justin does believe that part of his duty is to spread the word of God, which is a tenet of evangelical Christianity. While he does not think he should force his beliefs on anyone, he does feel it is appropriate for him to share his faith with his fans. "I feel I have an obligation to plant little seeds with my fans," he says. "I'm not going to tell them, 'You need Jesus,' but I will say at the end of my show, 'God loves you.'"[64] Still, part of Paramount Pictures' marketing effort for his biopic, *Never Say Never*, included screening the film for spiritual leaders across the country. In addition, the movie was distributed with a spiritual discussion guide. The guide suggests that the biopic "provides an opportunity to teach our children about the power of hope, prayer, faith and family."[65]

Diane Winston, who teaches media and religion at the University of Southern California, comments that celebrities often use "the language of faith to widen their audience and project a clean pop image. For young stars, particularly in those murky young teenage years, it's a quick, reliable way to show parents you are not going to be offering a sexually explicit message."[66] Mallette, who wrote the introduction for the resource guide, is not bothered by the implication that faith is being used as a marketing tool. "Faith is such a big part of our lives," she said. "You can't cut it out of the movie, so they might as well make it work for them."[67]

Charity Work

Justin feels it is his obligation as a Christian to use his celebrity to help others in need. Philanthropy is a key part of Justin's business plan. For example, the video for his song "Pray" combines his Christian values with a desire to help others by featuring footage from earthquake-ravaged Haiti and post-Katrina New Orleans. Justin donated the proceeds from his album *My World Acoustic* (which features the song "Pray") to the Children's Miracle Network. "I am in the position to give back thanks to my fans and God," said Bieber. "I wrote 'Pray' thinking I wanted to help others and I feel like I have a responsibility to do so. ... This album is a gift to my fans and the money raised from it allows us all to help out."[68]

Justin began his charity efforts early in his career. It was important to him that a charity component was written into every business deal. He has also used his influence to raise money for various causes. For example, he donated his sneakers to be auctioned off to benefit his school in Stratford and has since donated sneakers, as well as snippets of his hair, for other charitable auctions. On his

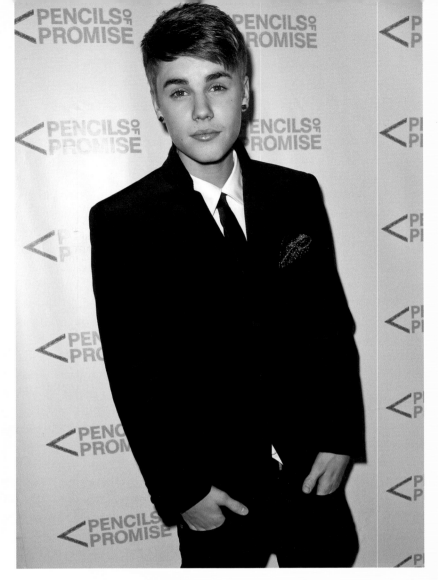

Justin became involved with charity work early in his career. One of his favorite charitable organizations is Pencils for Promise, which builds schools in less-developed countries.

seventeenth and eighteenth birthdays, he asked fans to donate seventeen and eighteen dollars, respectively, to support efforts to provide clean water to people in developing countries. In addition to playing numerous benefit concerts, he produced a line of nail polish

Adam Braun and Pencils of Promise

Adam Braun has always had a passion for education. He grew up with two adopted brothers from Mozambique, which taught both he and his brother, Scooter, that raising people up out of poverty was everyone's responsibility. Education is the best way he knows to do that.

After college, Braun took a finance job with the consulting firm Bain & Company so he could gain skills to start his own nonprofit. He traveled around Asia to learn what was needed, and he asked the children he met to tell him their wishes. Their answers surprised him: One wanted to dance, and another wanted a book. "When I got to India," he remembers, "that's where the poverty was most devastating—children begging on the street, carrying babies. ... The boy that I happened to ask in that country, he was probably 8 or 9 years old, begging on the street and he said he wanted a pencil. That was it."

Braun says he decided to start the organization Pencils of Promise "because that first pencil led to many pencils." He began raising money to build schools in developing nations. With the support of his brother and Justin Bieber, they have built nearly fifty schools.

Quoted in Shirley Halperin. "Adam Braun on Pencils of Promise and How Justin Bieber Is 'Making the World Better.'" *Hollywood Reporter*, July 28, 2011. www.hollywoodreporter.com/news/adam-braun-pencils-promise-how-216267.

and donated all proceeds to charity, and he still donates one dollar of every ticket sold to his favorite charity, Pencils of Promise.

Pencils of Promise is an organization run by Scooter Braun's brother, Adam, which builds schools in developing nations. The idea for donating a portion of ticket sales was Justin's, who asked his manager if they could give one dollar of every ticket on his *My World* tour to the organization. "I could see how smart Adam was," Justin said, "but it was about the cause for me. I'm young, Pencils of Promise is a young charity and it's helping young people with schooling and education, so I really wanted to be a part of that."[69] They raised enough money on the tour to build more than thirty schools. Since then Justin and Braun have used every opportunity to support the organization, with the goal of breaking ground on one hundred schools by the end of 2012.

In 2011 Justin won the number two spot on DoSomething.org's annual Celebs Gone Good list, which ranks celebrity philanthropic impact. His rank increased from number ten in 2010 in part because he began the Believe Charity Drive, which aimed to raise at least $1 million before the release of his album *Believe* in 2012. The charity supports efforts that emphasize education, well-being, youth, and music, and include Project Medishare for Haiti, the Boys & Girls Clubs of America, and the GRAMMY Foundation. He also donated a portion of the profits from his Christmas album *Under the Mistletoe* and his teen fragrance, Someday, to charitable organizations like the Make-A-Wish Foundation. He grants wishes for the organization as well, often spending an hour or so before his concerts with children whose wish is to meet Justin Bieber.

Despite all his philanthropic efforts, Justin was criticized in 2011 for not using enough of his influence to help worthy causes. *Forbes* did a study that put a dollar figure on a celebrity's ability to generate publicity and then compared it to the amount of publicity they actually generated for charitable causes. Justin's personal publicity value was estimated at $4.2 billion—the highest on the list—but when it came to how much he leveraged his influence, he came in last. Mark Iafrate, an analyst who developed the study's methodology, notes, "He's the perfect storm for generating high media value: lots of publicity in high impact sources, and an audience eager and able to spread that content. The amount of discussion, along with the quality of the sources, all push him way above everyone else. ... If he just spent a little more time on [causes], he could do a lot better."[70]

However, the study had some problems. It searched the Internet for instances of the celebrity's name appearing online, and then compared that to how many times that name was promoting philanthropic efforts. It allowed for variations of spellings and included Twitter handles in its search, which is one reason why Justin's publicity value was ranked so high—thousands of Twitter handles include variations of Justin's name but have nothing to do with the artist.

Justin continues to support causes close to his heart, and he hopes to increase his philanthropic work each year. One charity that is particularly special to him is the Stratford House of Blessing, the food bank that he and his mother used to visit from time to time when Justin was growing up. In November 2011 he donated enough money to the organization to stock its shelves through Christmas. That was something he had wanted to do since he was a boy. Helping others has always been important to Justin. "What is the point of doing all this," he asks, "if you can't make a difference in others' lives?"[71]

What's Next?

For Justin Bieber, the future looks bright. He is as popular as ever—the entire North American leg of his *Believe* tour, which began in September 2012, sold out in just one hour. He is interested in doing more acting and is working on a movie with Mark Wahlberg that will feature Justin as a basketball player. And while there are no marriage plans in the works between Justin and his girlfriend, Selena Gomez, he has repeatedly expressed the desire to marry and be a young dad. But his main focus will remain his music, at least for the time being. He wants to grow as a musician and performer, and he still views his favorite artist, Michael Jackson, as his idol.

Regardless of what the future holds for Justin, he is determined to tackle it head on. He says:

My goal at the end of the day—right now—I want to be successful and be great at what I do. But eventually, I want to become the best at what I do. I want to be the best. In the world. I want to be better than anybody that's ever done it. And in order to do that, I need to strive to be the best, be good to people and treat people with respect, and work as hard as I can. Because for me, I work so hard and this consumes my life, and it's not worth it if I'm not the best.[72]

Notes

Introduction: A Teen Idol for the New Millennium

1. Quoted in Joe LaPuma. "Justin Bieber: Second Round KO." *Complex*, March 19, 2012.

Chapter 1: A Rough Start

2. Quoted in *100 Huntley Street*. "Running from Pain and Finding Hope—Pattie Mallette." May 17, 2010. http://test.100huntley.com/video.php?id=NWozCvf2H5E.
3. Quoted in *100 Huntley Street*. "Running from Pain and Finding Hope—Pattie Mallette."
4. Quoted in *Justin Bieber: Never Say Never*. Directed by J. M. Chu. Hollywood, CA: Paramount Home Entertainment, 2011.
5. Quoted in Vanessa Grigoriadis. "The Adventures of Super Boy." *Rolling Stone*, March 3, 2011.
6. Quoted in Grigoriadis. "The Adventures of Super Boy."
7. Quoted in *E! Entertainment News Special*. "Justin Bieber: *My World*." E! Entertainment Television, July 7, 2010.
8. Quoted in *E! Entertainment News Special*. "Justin Bieber."
9. Quoted in *Justin Bieber*.
10. Quoted in *E! Entertainment News Special*. "Justin Bieber."
11. Quoted in Frazier Snowden. "Bieber Fever Hits Stratford." 106.9: The X, June 3, 2011. www.1069thex.com/news/bieber-fever-hits-stratford.
12. Justin Bieber. *First Step 2 Forever: My Story*. HarperCollins, 2010, p. 40.
13. Quoted in *E! Entertainment News Special*. "Justin Bieber."
14. Bieber. *First Step 2 Forever*, p. 41.

Chapter 2: The Kid Has It All

15. Quoted in Bieber. *First Step 2 Forever*, p. 60.
16. Quoted in *E! Entertainment News Special*. "Justin Bieber."

17. Quoted in *Justin Bieber.*
18. Quoted in Snowden. "Bieber Fever Hits Stratford."
19. Bieber. *First Step 2 Forever,* p. 56.
20. Quoted in Snowden. "Bieber Fever Hits Stratford."
21. Quoted in Snowden. "Bieber Fever Hits Stratford."
22. Quoted in *Justin Bieber.*
23. Bieber. *First Step 2 Forever,* p. 62.
24. Bieber. *First Step 2 Forever,* p. 81.
25. Quoted in *E! Entertainment News Special.* "Justin Bieber."
26. Bieber. *First Step 2 Forever,* pp. 88–89.
27. Bieber. *First Step 2 Forever,* pp. 91–92.

Chapter 3: From YouTube to Superstar

28. Quoted in Bieber. *First Step 2 Forever,* p. 110.
29. Bieber. *First Step 2 Forever,* p. 122.
30. Quoted in Jan Hoffman. "Justin Bieber Is Living the Tween Idol Dream." *New York Times,* January 3, 2010.
31. Bieber. *First Step 2 Forever,* pp. 125-126.
32. Quoted in Bieber. *First Step 2 Forever,* p. 144.
33. Bieber. *First Step 2 Forever,* p. 172.
34. Quoted in *Justin Bieber.*
35. Bieber. *First Step 2 Forever,* p. 188.

Chapter 4: The Image of a Superstar

36. Hoffman. "Justin Bieber Is Living the Tween Idol Dream."
37. Kiri Blakeley. "Justin Bieber's Days Are Numbered." *Forbes,* September 21, 2011. www.forbes.com/sites/kiriblakeley/2011/09/21/justin-biebers-days-are-numbered.
38. James Parker. "Daydream Belieber." *Atlantic,* March, 2011. www.theatlantic.com/magazine/archive/2011/03/daydream-believer/8374.
39. Quoted in *E! Entertainment News Special.* "Justin Bieber."
40. Bieber. *First Step 2 Forever,* p. 72.
41. Bieber. *First Step 2 Forever,* p. 76.

42. Justin Bieber. "Justin Bieber Screensaver." Video. Funny or Die. www.funnyordie.com/videos/a2c5a6fa8c/bieber-loves-you-girl?playlist=308176.

43. Quoted in Grigoriadis. "The Adventures of Super Boy."

44. Joy Behar. *The View*. ABC, February 17, 2011.

45. Quoted in Rebecca Macatee. "Back off Bieber! Writer of Controversial *Rolling Stone* Article Found Justin's Answers 'Sound and Logical.'" *PopEater*, February 17, 2011. www.popeater.com/2011/02/17/justin-bieber-rolling-stone-defense.

46. Quoted in *Extra*. "Justin Bieber Exclusive: Paternity Test Still On." Video. November 18, 2011. www.extratv.com/2011/11/18/justin-bieber-exclusive-paternity-test-still-on.

47. Quoted in *Extra*. "Justin Bieber Exclusive."

48. Quoted in LaPuma. "Justin Bieber."

Chapter 5: The Power of the Beliebers

49. Justin Bieber. Twitter. May 28, 2012. https://twitter.com/justinbieber.

50. Quoted in *Biebermania!* DVD. Directed by Thomas Gibson. Los Angeles: Lapdog Entertainment, 2011.

51. Quoted in Lisa Robinson. "The Kid Just Has It." *Vanity Fair*. February 2011.

52. Quoted in *Biebermania!*

53. Quoted in Hoffman. "Justin Bieber Is Living the Tween Idol Dream."

54. Regina Phalange. Twitter. May 25, 2012. https://twitter.com/BieberCrazyness.

55. Susan Clark. "Justin Bieber Tweets About Woman Who Claims He Fathered Her Baby." *Entertainment* (blog), ABC News, April 23, 2012. http://abcnews.go.com/blogs/entertainment/2012/04/justin-bieber-tweets-about-woman-who-claims-he-fathered-her-baby.

56. Quoted in Grigoriadis. "The Adventures of Super Boy."

57. Quoted in Katy Vine. "Girls Love Me." *Texas Monthly*, June 2, 2012.
58. Quoted in Grigoriadis. "The Adventures of Super Boy."

Chapter 6: Christian Charity

59. Quoted in Elliott David. "Watch the Throne." *V*, Summer 2012.
60. Quoted in Tim Townsend. "Bieber Documentary Taps Into Christian Audience." *Chicago Tribune*, February 16, 2011.
61. Quoted in David. "Watch the Throne."
62. Quoted in David. "Watch the Throne."
63. Quoted in David. "Watch the Throne."
64. Quoted in Grigoriadis. "The Adventures of Super Boy."
65. Paramount Pictures. *Discussion Guide: Never Say Never … for Nothing Is Impossible with God.* Hollywood: Paramount Pictures, 2011. http://media.salemwebnetwork.com/godtube/documents/neversaynever.pdf.
66. Quoted in Piet Levy. "Tween Evangelist?" *USA Today*, February 10, 2011.
67. Quoted in Townsend. "Bieber Documentary Taps Into Christian Audience."
68. Quoted in Business Wire. "Fresh off the AMAs: Artist of the Year Justin Bieber Donating Portion of Proceeds of New Album to Children's Miracle Network." November 24, 2010. www.businesswire.com/news/home/20101124005933/en/Fresh-AMAs-Artist-Year-Justin-Bieber-Donating.
69. Quoted in Shirley Halperin. "Adam Braun on Pencils of Promise and How Justin Bieber Is 'Making the World Better.'" *Hollywood Reporter*, July 28, 2011. www.hollywoodreporter.com/news/adam-braun-pencils-promise-how-216267.
70. Quoted in Zack O'Malley Greenburg. "The Most Valuable Celebrity Relationships." *Forbes*, November 20, 2011.
71. Quoted in Business Wire. "Fresh off the AMAs."
72. Quoted in David. "Watch the Throne."

1994

Justin Drew Bieber is born on March 1 to Pattie Mallette and Jeremy Bieber.

2000–2001

Starts first grade Jeanne Sauvé Catholic School; plays the drums, piano, and guitar; joins the Youth Ice Hockey League in his hometown of Stratford, Ontario.

2002–2003

Has his first experience busking on the sidewalk with his *djembe*; friends organize the Justin Bieber Benefit Concert to raise money to purchase him an adult drum kit; is invited to play drums with an adult jazz band at local festival venues.

2007

Performs in Stratford Star talent competition and posts performances on YouTube; talent manager Scott "Scooter" Braun contacts Mallette about representing Justin and flies the family to Atlanta; Usher Raymond becomes Justin's comanager.

2008

Signs with Island Def Jam Music Group in April; moves to Atlanta, Georgia; records first studio album, *My World*.

2009

Releases four singles from first album, *My World*, and becomes the first solo artist in history to have four singles in the top forty of the *Billboard* Hot 100 chart prior to the release of a debut album; embarks on promotional tour, visiting U.S. radio stations, touring in Canada, and opening for Taylor Swift in the United Kingdom; breaks foot during concert at Wembley Arena in London; releases

My Word in November; performs at Christmas in Washington concert for President Barack Obama.

2010

Second album, *My World 2.0*, is released in February; embarks on *My World* word tour; begins dating pop singer and actress Selena Gomez; television appearances include *Saturday Night Live*, *The X Factor*, and *CSI: Crime Scene Investigation*; releases a compilation album, *My World Acoustic*; releases his memoir, *First Step 2 Forever: My Story*.

2011

Releases a biopic documentary, *Justin Bieber: Never Say Never*, and a compilation album, *Never Say Never: The Remixes*; controversial interview in *Rolling Stone* magazine is published; appears again on *Saturday Night Live* and *The X Factor*; accused of fathering Mariah Yeater's child; releases a Christmas album, *Under the Mistletoe*.

2012

Paternity suit is dropped; releases third studio album, *Believe*; embarks on *Believe* world tour. Second autobiography *Justin Bieber: Just Getting Started* is published in September.

For More Information

Books

Justin Bieber. *Justin Bieber: Just Getting Started.* HarperCollins, 2012. Another autobiography detailing life on tour, behind-the-scenes stories, and many photographs.

Justin Bieber. *First Step 2 Forever: My Story*. New York: HarperCollins, 2010. Autobiography describing Justin Bieber's early life and rise to fame.

Riley Brooks. *Justin Bieber: His World*. New York: Scholastic, 2010. Examines Justin Bieber's early life and career.

Pattie Mallette and A.J. Gregory. *Nowhere But Up: The Story of Justin Bieber's Mom.* Ada, MI: Revell, 2012. Pattie Mallette's biography.

Marc Shapiro. *Justin Bieber: The Fever!* New York: St. Martin's, 2010. A detailed, critical look at the Justin Bieber phenomenon.

Periodicals

Elliot David. "Watch the Throne." *V*, Spring 2012.

Zack O'Malley Greenburg. "Justin Bieber, Venture Capitalist." *Forbes*, June 4, 2012.

Vanessa Grigoriadis. "The Adventures of Super Boy." *Rolling Stone*, March 3, 2011.

Jan Hoffman. "Justin Bieber Is Living the Teen Idol Dream." *New York Times*, January 3, 2010.

Joe LaPuma. "Justin Bieber: Second Round KO." *Complex*, March 19, 2012.

Alex Morris. "Justin Bieber Can Hear Them Scream." *New Yorker*, August 1, 2010.

Lisa Robinson. "The Kid Just Has It." *Vanity Fair*, February 2011.

David W. Stowe. "Jesus Christ Rock Star." *New York Times*, April 23, 2011.

Katy Vine. "Girls Love Me." *Texas Monthly*, June 2, 2012.

Documentaries

Biebermania! DVD. Directed by Thomas Gibson. Los Angeles: Lapdog Entertainment, 2011.

E! Entertainment News Special. "Justin Bieber: *My World*." E! Entertainment Television, July 7, 2010.

Justin Bieber: Never Say Never. Directed by J. M. Chu. Hollywood, CA: Paramount Home Entertainment, 2011.

Websites

Justin Bieber, *Billboard.com* (www.billboard.com/artist/justin-bieber/1099520#/artist/justin-bieber/1099520). A comprehensive list of Justin Bieber's music and its history on the *Billboard* charts.

Justin Bieber, IMDb (www.imdb.com/name/nm3595501). A comprehensive list of all movie and television appearances by Justin Bieber.

Justin Bieber, MTV.com (www.mtv.com/music/artist/bieber_justin/artist.jhtml). Up-to-date information on Justin Bieber news, performances, and appearances.

Justin Bieber, Music.com (www.justinbiebermusic.com). The official Justin Bieber website. Includes information on the Believe Charity Drive.

Justin Bieber, YouTube (www.youtube.com/user/kidrauhl). An up-to-date collection of videos uploaded by Justin Bieber.

Justin Bieber Zone (www.justinbieberzone.com). The first and most comprehensive Justin Bieber fan site.

A

Acting, 53, 83

Albums
    Believe, 63, 71, 75
    My World, 8, 48, 49–50
    My World 2.0, 53
    My World Acoustic, 62, 79
    Never Say Never: The Remixes, 62
    number sold (2009–2012), 63
    Under the Mistletoe, 62–63, 82

"All Around the World" (song), 71

American Idol (television program), 33, *33*

Appearance, 9, 67

Atlanta, Georgia, 39, 46

Avon Theater, *29,* 31, 36–37

Awards and honors
    Billboard, 49, 53, 63
    Celebs Gone Good list, 82
    Forbes powerful celebrities, 63
    Grammy loss to Spaulding, 72
    Twitter, 71

B

"Baby" (song), 53

Beatles, compared to, 8, 67

Beliebers. *See* Fans

Believe (album), 63, 71, 75

Believe (tour), 83

Believe Charity Drive, 82

Bieber, Jeremy (father)
    Mallette (mother) and, 15, 16
    music, 27
    relationship with Justin, 22–23

Bieber, Justin, *9, 38, 43, 48, 52, 56, 61,*
    62, 68, 73, 80

Bieber Fever, 8, 49

Bilingualism, 26

Billboard
    200 chart, 53
    albums number 1 at debut, 63
    Hot 100 chart, 49

Biopic, 57, *77,* 79

Birth, 15

Boys & Girls Clubs of America, 82

Braun, Scott "Scooter," *40*

    advice to Justin, 42
    background, 39, 41
    biopic, 57
    discovery of Justin, 10
    fans of Justin, 73
    first meeting, 39–42
    Justin's transition to adult image, 63
    maintaining characteristics of Justin,
        55, 57–58
    marketing strategy, 46–48, 50, 57,
        67–68
    partnership with Usher, 44
    Pencils of Promise charity, 81–82
    threat of legal action against Yeater,
        59–60

Bubblegum pop, 51

Bullying, 11, 22

Busking
    by Avon Theater, 31, 36–37
    described, 30, *30*
    first time, 28

C

Canada, 26

Celebs Gone Good list, 82

Characteristics
    competitiveness, 25, 35
    drive and determination, 24, 35
    love being center of attention, 25–26, 31
    natural talent, 34, 35
    trouble in school, 32
    of typical fans, 64–65, 67–70

Charity work
    auctions, 79–80
    benefit concerts, 80
    causes supported, 11, 79, 80,
        81–82, 83
    as Christian obligation, 57, 79
    criticism of, as insufficient, 82–83
    donations requested from fans, 80
    Michael Jackson and, 57
    proceeds from albums, 79, 82
    proceeds from product lines, 62,
        80–81, 82
    by Usher, 45

Childhood
    busking, 28, *30, 30*–31, 36–37
    father during, 16, 22–23
    grandparents, 18, 20, 25
    living conditions, 16, 18
    music during, 20–22
    sports, 22, 24–26, *25*
Christianity
    beliefs and actions, 11, 22, 55,
        78–79
    charity work, 57, 79
    church attendance, 76
    Mallette (mother) as born-again
        Christian, 11, 14–15
    spiritual guide with biopic, 79
Christmas in Washington concert, 53
Chu, John, 57
Combs, Sean "P. Diddy," 45
Complex (magazine) cover, 63
A Concert for Hurricane Relief, 45
Concerts
    benefits, 31, 80
    described, 69
    opener for Taylor Swift, 52–53
    Oslo, 8, 70

D
Dale, Bruce (grandfather)
    busking by Justin, 36–37
    Justin on drums, 31
    relationship with Justin, 18, 20
    support for sports, 25
Dale, Diane (grandmother), 18, 20, 25
Dating, 61, *61*
*Dick Clark's New Year's Rockin' Eve with
    Ryan Seacrest* (television program), 53
Djembe, 21, *21,* 28
Documentary movie, 57
Dosomething.org, 82
Drums, 20–22, *21,* 31
Dupri, Jermaine, 40–41

E
Earnings
    donated to charity, 62, 79, 80–81, 82
    sources, 75
    2010-2011, 63
Education
    charities supporting, 81–82
    elementary school, 24

secondary school, 32
    tutor in Atlanta, 46
    voice coach, 46
Extra (television program), 59

F
Facebook, 47–48
"Fallin" (Keys), 34
Fans, *64, 68, 71*
    characteristics of typical, 8, 64–65,
        67–70
    developing, before digital era, 65
    digital backlash to increase in, 54
    digital communication with, 10–11,
        49, 68–69, 72
    donations to charities requested of, 80
    Justin's trust of, 73
    name for, 8, 64
    negative acts by, 72
    older women, 53, 70
    of other stars, 64, 66, 71, 74
    reaction to dating Gomez, 61
    sharing Christianity with, 78–79
    use of Internet to increase number,
        37, 39, 42, 65–67, 71
    websites developed by, 70
Fey, Tina, 53
First Step 2 Forever: My Story, 55, *56,* 57
Forbes (magazine), 59, 63, 82
French Canadians, 26
French language, 24, 26
Friends, 24, 32

G
Gomez, Selena, 54, 61, *61,* 83
Grammy award to Spaulding, 72
GRAMMY Foundation, 82

H
Hairstyle, 9
Haiti, 79, 82
Hockey, 24, *25*
The Hungarian Conflict (film), 41
Hurricane Katrina, 45

I
Image
    abortion/rape comments, 58–59
    efforts to maintain real, 55, 57–58
    examples of other artists, 51

media beliefs, 51, 54
paternity claim, 59–60, *60, 62*
transition to adult, 63
Internet
  backlash to increase in popularity, 54
  communication with fans, 10–11, 49,
    68–69, 72
  discovery on, 10
  fan websites, 70
  music industry and, 39, 65, 75
  power, 50
  promotional use, 37, 39, 42, 65–67,
    70, 71
  sale of songs, 10
  See also specific sites
Island Def Jam Music Group, 44, 46
It Gets Better project, 11
iTunes, 46–48

J
Jackson, Michael, *19,* 57, 83
Justin Bieber Benefit Concert, 31

K
Kardashian, Kim, 72, *73*
Kaye, Allison, 67
Keys, Alicia, 34

L
Lady Gaga, 51, 64, 71
LaFace Records, 45

M
Mahone, Austin, 74, *74,* 75
Make-A-Wish Foundation, 82
Mallette, Pattie (mother), *13*
  adolescence, 14
  adult fans of Justin, 53, 70
  beliefs about music industry, 39
  Braun and, 39–42
  busking by Justin, 36–37
  childhood, 12–13
  Justin and religion, 76–77
  music, 20
  religion, 11, 14–15, 79
  as single mother, 12, 16, 18, 83
  Stratford Star talent competition, 34, 35
Malloy, David, 75
Matchbox 20, 34

McKay, Nathan
  busking, 28, *29, 30,* 30–31
  Justin Bieber Benefit Concert, 31
  as mentor, 20, 22, 27
  Stratford blues festival, 17
Media
  opinion, 51, 53–54
  radio, 48–49
Music
  characteristics needed for career, 24
  drums, 20–22, *21*
  evangelic, 78
  instruments played, 20–22, *21,* 28
  learning by example, 27–28
  mentors, 20, 22, 27–28
  natural ability, 20, 22, 28
  Stratford festivals, 17
  as way to meet girls, 37
  See also Albums; Songs
Music industry
  effect of Internet, 39, 65, 75
  first contract, 46
  importance of teenagers, 67
  Justin as product, 51, 53–54
  labels of Braun, 41, 44
  Mallette's beliefs about, 39
My World (album), 8, 48, 49–50
My World 2.0 (album), 53
My World Acoustic (album), 62, 79

N
Never Say Never (biopic), *77,* 79
Never Say Never: The Remixes (album), 62
New Look Foundation, 45
New York Times (newspaper), 51

O
Obama, Barack, 53
"One Less Lonely Girl" (song), 70
"One Time" (song and video), 46–48
"100th Digital Short" (television skit), 53
Oprah (television program), 53
Oslo, Norway concert, 8, 70, *71*

P
Paternity claim controversy, 59–60, *60,*
  62, 72
Pencils of Promise charity, 81–82
Perfume, 62, 82

Poverty during childhood, 16, 18
"Pray" (video and song), 79
Project Medishare for Haiti, 82
Prophetic word reading, 76–77
Public assistance, 16

R
Radio stations, 48–49
Raymond, Usher Terry. *See* Usher
Raymond-Braun Media Group, 41
Reid, L.A., 44, 45, 46
Religion. *See* Christianity
"Respect" (Otis Redding song), 34
Role models, 11, 57, 83
Rolling Stone (magazine), 58
Romance
    appeal to fans, 69–70
    Gomez, Selena, 54, 61, *61,* 83
    Kardashian, Kim, 72

S
Saturday Night Live (television
    program), 53
School Boy Records, 41, 44
School of Young Performers, 46
Selena Gomez & the Scene, 61
Shakespeare Festival, 17, *17*
Smith, Jan, 46
So So Def Recordings, 41
Someday (perfume), 82
Songs
    "All Around the World," 71
    "Baby," 53
    "One Less Lonely Girl," 70
    "One Time," 46–48
    "Pray," 79
    sold on Internet, 10
    "U Smile," 53
    writers, 46
Soulja Boy, 75
Spaulding, Esperanza, 72
Sports, 22, 24, 25
Springsteen, Bruce, 51
Stafford Northwestern Secondary
    School, 32
Star Search (television program), 44, 45
Stratford, Ontario (Canada), 16, *16,* 17
Stratford House of Blessing, 83

Stratford Star talent competition, 33–35
Street performances, 28, *29, 30,* 30–31
Suicide attempt of mother, 14
Swift, Taylor, 52

T
Television appearances, 53
Texas Monthly (magazine), 75
Texting, 11
"3 AM" (Matchbox 20 song), 34
Timberlake, Justin, 44
Time (magazine), 69
Tolerance, 22
Twitter, *47*
    direct communication with fans,
        10–11, 68–69
    Mahone following, 75
    most followed person, 71
    promotions, 47–48, 49

U
"U Smile" (song), 53
Under the Mistletoe (album), 62–63, 82
Usher, *43, 45*
    background of, 45
    full name, 10
    meeting, 40–41
    partnership with Braun, 44
    songs for Justin, 46

V
Video, 46–48
The View (television program), 58

W
Wahlberg, Mark, 83
Way, DeAndre Cortez, 75

Y
Yeater, Mariah, 59–60, *60,* 62, 72
YouTube
    discovery on, 10
    growth of fan base, 37, 39, 42
    Mahone, Austin, 74
    music industry recognition, 39
    music industry videos, 75
    Stratford Star talent competition, 35

Picture Credits

About the Author

Christine Wilcox is a writer and editor. She studied literature at Temple University and received an MA in English from the University of Maine. Wilcox is a certified instructional designer and has published fiction and nonfiction in various journals. She lives in Richmond, Virginia, with her husband, David, and her stepson, Anthony.